T0215526

Advanced Perl Programming

From Advanced to Expert

William "Bo" Rothwell

Apress®

Advanced Perl Programming: From Advanced to Expert

William "Bo" Rothwell
El Cajon, CA, USA

ISBN-13 (pbk): 978-1-4842-5862-0   ISBN-13 (electronic): 978-1-4842-5863-7
https://doi.org/10.1007/978-1-4842-5863-7

Copyright © 2020 by William "Bo" Rothwell of One Course Source, Inc.

This work is subject to copyright. All rights are reserved by the Publisher, whether the whole or part of the material is concerned, specifically the rights of translation, reprinting, reuse of illustrations, recitation, broadcasting, reproduction on microfilms or in any other physical way, and transmission or information storage and retrieval, electronic adaptation, computer software, or by similar or dissimilar methodology now known or hereafter developed.

Trademarked names, logos, and images may appear in this book. Rather than use a trademark symbol with every occurrence of a trademarked name, logo, or image we use the names, logos, and images only in an editorial fashion and to the benefit of the trademark owner, with no intention of infringement of the trademark.

The use in this publication of trade names, trademarks, service marks, and similar terms, even if they are not identified as such, is not to be taken as an expression of opinion as to whether or not they are subject to proprietary rights.

While the advice and information in this book are believed to be true and accurate at the date of publication, neither the authors nor the editors nor the publisher can accept any legal responsibility for any errors or omissions that may be made. The publisher makes no warranty, express or implied, with respect to the material contained herein.

Managing Director, Apress Media LLC: Welmoed Spahr
Acquisitions Editor: Steve Anglin
Development Editor: Matthew Moodie
Coordinating Editor: Mark Powers

Cover designed by eStudioCalamar

Cover image by Lukas Spitaler on Unsplash (www.unsplash.com)

Distributed to the book trade worldwide by Springer Science+Business Media New York, 233 Spring Street, 6th Floor, New York, NY 10013. Phone 1-800-SPRINGER, fax (201) 348-4505, e-mail orders-ny@springer-sbm.com, or visit www.springeronline.com. Apress Media, LLC is a California LLC and the sole member (owner) is Springer Science + Business Media Finance Inc (SSBM Finance Inc). SSBM Finance Inc is a **Delaware** corporation.

For information on translations, please e-mail editorial@apress.com; for reprint, paperback, or audio rights, please email bookpermissions@springernature.com.

Apress titles may be purchased in bulk for academic, corporate, or promotional use. eBook versions and licenses are also available for most titles. For more information, reference our Print and eBook Bulk Sales web page at http://www.apress.com/bulk-sales.

Any source code or other supplementary material referenced by the author in this book is available to readers on GitHub via the book's product page, located at www.apress.com/9781484258620. For more detailed information, please visit http://www.apress.com/source-code.

Printed on acid-free paper

To all Perl Mongers, new and old.

Table of Contents

About the Author

At the impressionable age of 14, **William "Bo" Rothwell** crossed paths with a TRS-80 Micro Computer System (affectionately known as a "Trash 80"). Soon after, the adults responsible for Bo made the mistake of leaving him alone with the TRS-80. He immediately dismantled it and held his first computer class, showing his friends what made this "computer thing" work. Since this experience, Bo's passion for understanding how computers work and sharing this knowledge with others has resulted in a rewarding career in IT training. His experience includes Linux, Unix, DevOps tools, orchestration, security, and programming languages such as Perl, Python, Tcl, and Bash.

Bo can be contacted via LinkedIn: www.linkedin.com/in/bo-rothwell.

About the Technical Reviewer

Massimo Nardone has more than 24 years of experience in security, web and mobile development, and cloud and IT architecture. His true IT passions are security and Android.

He has been programming and teaching how to program with Android, Perl, PHP, Java, VB, Python, C/C++, and MySQL for more than 20 years.

He holds a Master of Science degree in Computing Science from the University of Salerno, Italy.

He has worked as a project manager, software engineer, research engineer, chief security architect, information security manager, PCI/SCADA auditor, and senior lead IT security/cloud/SCADA architect for many years.

His technical skills include security, Android, cloud, Java, MySQL, Drupal, Cobol, Perl, web and mobile development, MongoDB, D3, Joomla, Couchbase, C/C++, WebGL, Python, Pro Rails, Django CMS, Jekyll, Scratch, and so on.

He worked as a visiting lecturer and supervisor for exercises at the Networking Laboratory of the Helsinki University of Technology (Aalto University). He holds four international patents (PKI, SIP, SAML, and Proxy areas).

He currently works as chief information security officer (CISO) for Cargotec Oyj, and he is a member of ISACA Finland Chapter Board.

Massimo has reviewed more than 45 IT books for different publishers and has coauthored *Pro JPA in Java EE 8* (Apress, 2018), *Beginning EJB in Java EE 8* (Apress, 2018), and *Pro Spring Security* (Apress, 2019).

Acknowledgments

Thanks to all of the folks at Apress for helping me get this book to print:

- Steve: Thanks for getting the ball rolling.

- Matthew: Appreciate your "behind the scenes" guidance.

- Mark: Great job keeping this project on track.

- Massimo: Excellent work providing useful technical feedback.

CHAPTER 1

Command-Line Options

Perl command-line options aren't necessarily an "advanced" topic. However, with the exception of a couple of common options, most Perl programmers don't explore command-line options until they have been working with Perl for a while. This is unfortunate as some of the command-line options provide some very useful features.

This chapter won't cover every command-line option. It will focus on some of the most useful options. The following chart contains a brief summary of most of Perl's command-line options:

Option	Meaning
--	Terminates options
-0[octalnum]	Specifies the input record separator as an octal character
-a	Turns on autosplit if used with the -n or -p options
-c	Checks syntax only
-d	Executes Perl using the debugger
-Dnumber	Sets debugging flags
-e 'perl cmd'	Executes code listed on command line
-F/pattern/	Specifies what pattern to split on when -a is used
-h	Displays a summary of command-line options
-i[ext]	Tells Perl to edit files that are processed by <> in place
-Idir	Specifies what directories to pre-append to the @INC array
-l[octnum]	Enables automatic line-end processing
-Mmodule	Executes "use module" before running your script
-n	Executes a while loop around your script
-p	Executes a while loop around your script

© William "Bo" Rothwell of One Course Source, Inc. 2020
W. "Bo" Rothwell, *Advanced Perl Programming*, https://doi.org/10.1007/978-1-4842-5863-7_1

Option	Meaning
-P	Runs your script through the C preprocessor before compiling
-s	Provides simple parsing of command-line options and arguments
-S	Searches PATH variables to search for script
-T	Turns on taint checks
-u	Creates core dump file after compiling
-U	Allows unsafe operations
-v	Displays version of Perl
-V	Displays configuration information of Perl
-w	Prints warnings during executing about possible logical errors
-x [*dir*]	Extracts scripts embedded in a message

Changing input record separator

Note   In the *Beginning Perl Programming: From Novice to Professional* book, we covered how to change the input record separator. This is a brief review of what was covered.

The "record separator variable" stores the character(s) that Perl uses to "break up" the data that is read by <STDIN> (or any filehandle).

The record separator variable name is **$/**. By default, it is set to a new line character ("\n").

Suppose we had a database file which contained a completely flat database:

Ted:9930:accounting:Bob:9940:HR:Sue:9950:accounting:

In this case, we could change the **$/** variable to a colon (":") and read the entire file into an array with each element being a field in the array:

```
$/=":";
@fields=<STDIN>;
chomp (@fields);
$/="\n";
```

Notes:

- The **chomp** command actually chomps whatever the **$/** variable is set to.

- It's important to set the **$/** variable to its previous value as soon as you are finished reading the file. This is because this is a truly global variable and making changes to it could affect other portions of the script.

With the **-0** (zero) option, you can change the input record separator on the command line. The value you specify has to be in octal format. On a UNIX system, you can view octal numbers by looking at the ASCII table:

```
[student@ocs student]$ man ascii
|040 SP |041  !  |042  "  |043  #  |044  $  |045  %  |
|046  &  |047  '  |050  (  |051  )  |052  *  |053  +  |
|054  ,  |055  -  |056  .  |057  /  |060  0  |061  1  |
|062  2  |063  3  |064  4  |065  5  |066  6  |067  7  |
|070  8  |071  9  |072  :  |073  ;  |074  <  |075  =  |
|076  >  |077  ?  |100  @  |101  A  |102  B  |103  C  |
|104  D  |105  E  |106  F  |107  G  |110  H  |111  I  |
|112  J  |113  K  |114  L  |115  M  |116  N  |117  O  |
|120  P  |121  Q  |122  R  |123  S  |124  T  |125  U  |
|126  V  |127  W  |130  X  |131  Y  |132  Z  |133  [  |
|134  \  |135  ]  |136  ^  |137  _  |140  `  |141  a  |
|142  b  |143  c  |144  d  |145  e  |146  f  |147  g  |
|150  h  |151  i  |152  j  |153  k  |154  l  |155  m  |
|156  n  |157  o  |160  p  |161  q  |162  r  |163  s  |
|164  t  |165  u  |166  v  |167  w  |170  x  |171  y  |
|172  z  |173  {  |174  |  |175  }  |176  ~  |177 DEL|
```

Notes:

- On other systems, you can perform a Google search to display the ASCII text table.

- If the value 00 is used, Perl will read in a paragraph at a time.

- If the value 0777 is used, $/ is set to **undef** which causes Perl to read the entire file the first time the filehandle is read.

Example:

```perl
#!perl
#sep.pl
#Note: assumes script was run with -0 option

open (NAMES, "<names.txt") || die;
@people=<NAMES>;
chomp (@people);
print "First name in list: $people[0]\n";
close NAMES;
```

Output of sep.pl:

```
[student@ocs student]$ perl -0072 sep.pl
First name in list: Bob
```

Create a loop around your script

When you use the **-n** option, Perl places the following loop around your code:

```perl
while (<>) {
    #Your code here
}
```

In the *Beginning Perl Programming: From Novice to Professional* book, we covered the diamond operator, <>. This operator will read from files that are specified on the command line. If no files are specified, the diamond operator reads from STDIN.

In the following example, the script will display the lines that are read from <> with the line number preceding it:

```perl
#!perl
#loop1.pl

print "$. $_";
```

In order for this to work, you will either need to execute Perl with the **-n** option

```
[student@ocs student]$ perl -n loop1.pl file.txt
```

or include the **-n** option in the magic cookie line:

```
#!perl -n
```

Example output of `loop1.pl`:

```
[student@ocs student]$ perl -n loop1.pl local.cshrc
1 # @(#)cshrc 1.11 89/11/29 SMI
2 umask 022
3 set path=(/bin /usr/bin /usr/ucb /etc .)
4 if ( $?prompt ) then
5     set history=32
6 endif
```

You can also use the **-n** option in conjunction with the **-e** option:

```
[student@ocs student]$ perl -n -e 'print "$. $_";' local.cshrc
1 # @(#)cshrc 1.11 89/11/29 SMI
2 umask 022
3 set path=(/bin /usr/bin /usr/ucb /etc .)
4 if ( $?prompt ) then
5     set history=32
6 endif
```

Note   On Windows-based systems, the **print** statement must be placed within double quotes as required by the shell interface.

Looping and printing

The **-n** option and the **-p** option are almost the same. The only difference is that, by default, **-n** produces no output, while the **-p** option prints the **$_** variable at the end of the **while** loop.

In the following example, the file listed on the command line will be capitalized and the outcome printed to STDOUT:

```
#!perl -p
#loop2.pl

tr/a-z/A-Z/;
```

Example output of loop2.pl:

```
[student@ocs student]$ loop2.pl local.cshrc
# @(#)CSHRC 1.11 89/11/29 SMI
UMASK 022
SET PATH=(/BIN /USR/BIN /USR/UCB /ETC .)
IF ( $?PROMPT ) THEN
        SET HISTORY=32
ENDIF
```

Looping and parsing

When you use the **-a** option in conjunction with the **-p** or **-n** option, Perl will automatically run the **split** command on the **$_** variable. The **split** command will split on a space (" ") and place the results in the **@F** array:

```
#!perl -a -n
#auto1.pl

print "$F[0] \n";
```

Example output of auto1.pl:

```
[student@ocs student]$ auto1.pl auto.txt
This
for
to
of
```

If you want the split to be done on a different character than a space, use the **-F** option. The argument to the **-F** option can be either a quoted (double or single) string or a regular expression (surrounded by //):

```
[student@ocs student]$ perl -a -n -F":" auto1.pl group
root
other
bin
```

```
sys
adm
uucp
mail
tty
lp
nuucp
staff
daemon
sysadmin
smmsp
nobody
noaccess
nogroup
```

Note   Because of the way the magic cookie is parsed, these options (**-a** and **-F**) may not perform correctly when used in the magic cookie.

Editing in place

You can modify an existing file "in place" when you use the **-i** option in conjunction with the **-p** option. The **-i** option tells Perl to "print" back to the file instead of STDOUT.

Perl also allows you the option to automatically create a backup of the original file. By adding an extension argument to the **-i** option, Perl will modify the original file after making a backup of it.

The following example will capitalize the text in the file that is listed as an argument on the command line and make a backup file called "file.orig":

```
#!perl -p -i.orig
#edit1.pl

tr/a-z/A-Z/;
```

Flexibility in backup filenames

You can also use the "*" character to represent the filename itself. For example, the following program will name the backup file old.FILENAME:

```
#!perl -p -iold.*
#edit2.pl

tr/a-z/A-Z/;
```

Backing up to different directories

You can even specify to the **-i** option that you want to back up to a different directory:

```
perl -p -i '/var/backup/*.old' script.pl filename.txt
```

If you don't supply an argument to the **-i** option, Perl will produce the following error message: "Can't do inplace edit without backup".

Syntax checking

If you want to perform syntax checking only on a script, use the **-c** option. Perl will compile the code and then exit your script. This would be similar to putting the statement "exit 0" as the first line of code in your script.

While Perl won't execute code listed in the main part of your program (or any functions either), there is some code that could be executed. If you have a BEGIN block in your code, these statements will be executed. In addition, any code wrapped within a **use** statement will be executed as well.

We will discuss BEGIN blocks in more detail in a future Unit. In a nutshell, BEGIN blocks are used to execute initialization code during compile time.

There are also END blocks in Perl that are commonly used to perform "clean up" actions. END blocks are not executed when the **-c** option is used. However, if you use the "exit 0" method mentioned earlier, END blocks would be executed.

Example output:

```
[student@ocs student]$ perl -c syntax1.pl
syntax1.pl syntax OK
[student@ocs student]$ perl -c syntax2.pl
Can't find string terminator '"' anywhere before EOF at syntax2.pl line 4.
```

Pre-appending to @INC

In the *Pro Perl Programming: From Professional to Advanced* book, we covered how to modify the **@INC** array during the compile stage. The following section is a review of that topic.

Manipulate @INC at compile time

If you install your own modules, you may not be able to put them in one of the default locations. Typically, only the system administrator can modify these directories.

In such cases, you will want to modify the **@INC** variable during compile time. To do this, use the **lib** pragma:

```
#!perl
#lib.pl

use lib "perl_class";

print "@INC", "\n";
```

The argument to the "**use lib**" statement will be pre-appended to the **@INC** variable.

Using the -I option

In addition to the **use lib** statement, you can pre-append to the **@INC** array by using the **-I** (Capital "i") option:

```
[student@ocs student]$ perl -I "perl_class" script.pl
```

Including modules

In previous books in this series (*Beginning Perl Programming: From Novice to Professional* and *Pro Perl Programming: From Professional to Advanced*), we covered how to import modules by using the **use** statement. You can also import modules with the command-line option **-M**. For example, if the following code

```
#!perl
#mod1.pl

print hostname;
```

is executed like this:

```
[student@ocs student]$ perl -MSys::Hostname mod1.pl
```

then the statement "print hostname" will display the outcome of the function "hostname" that was imported from the Sys::Hostname module.

Using -M to load specific identifiers from modules

Suppose you only want to import certain variables and functions from a module. If you were including the code in the file itself, you could write it like this:

```
use Text::Wrap qw(wrap $columns);
```

To do this via the command line, use the **-M** option. For example, if the following code is executed

```
#!perl
#mod2.pl

$line="This is an example of how you can break up text into formatted
paragraphs.  This process is done by professionals on a closed track. Don't
attempt this at home!";

$columns=40;
print wrap ("\t", "", $line);
print "\n";
```

using this command line

```
[student@ocs student]$ perl '-MText::Wrap qw(wrap $columns)' mod2.pl
```

then Perl will only import the "wrap" function and the "$columns" variable from the Text::Wrap module.

Alternative syntax to -M

There is an alternative, easier to read (and write) method to the **-M** option. Instead of running the preceding script like this:

```
[student@ocs student]$ perl '-MText::Wrap qw(wrap $columns)' mod2.pl
```

it could have been written like this:

```
[student@ocs student]$ perl '-MText::Wrap=wrap,$columns' mod2.pl
```

Command-line parsing

The **-s** option provides some basic command-line parsing of the options and arguments being sent to your script. For each command-line option sent to your script, the **-s** option will do the following:

1. Create a variable that contains the same name as the option

2. Set this variable to "1" if no argument follows the variable

3. Remove the option (and argument if there is one) from the @ARGV array

Example:

```perl
#!perl -s
#arg1.pl

if ($p) {print "Output will be sent to printer\n";}

if ($c) {print "Full syntax checking turned on\n";}

print "@ARGV", "\n";
```

Example output of `arg1.pl`:

```
[student@ocs student]$ arg.pl -p -c file.txt sample.old
Output will be sent to printer
Full syntax checking turned on
file.txt sample.old
```

If you want to use arguments with your options, you have to use the syntax **-option=argument**. In this case, Perl will assign the value of the argument to the variable name "option":

```
#!perl -s
#arg2.pl

print "$directory\n";
```

Example output of `arg2.pl`:

```
[student@ocs student]$ arg2.pl -directory=/junk
/junk
```

Note   The **-s** option isn't a very advanced parser. If you want something more complex, you will need to handle it manually or use a module like Getopt::Std or Getopt::Long.

Displaying configuration information

The **-V** option displays a summary of Perl's configuration data. The following example is from a Windows-based system with Strawberry Perl:

```
C:\Windows\System32> perl -V
```

Summary of my perl5 (revision 5 version 30 subversion 1) configuration:

```
Platform:
  osname=MSWin32
  osvers=10.0.18363.476
```

```
archname=MSWin32-x64-multi-thread
uname='Win32 strawberry-perl 5.30.1.1 #1 Fri Nov 22 02:24:29 2019 x64'
config_args='undef'
hint=recommended
useposix=true
d_sigaction=undef
useithreads=define
usemultiplicity=define
use64bitint=define
use64bitall=undef
uselongdouble=undef
usemymalloc=n
default_inc_excludes_dot=define
bincompat5005=undef
Compiler:
cc='gcc'
ccflags =' -s -O2 -DWIN32 -DWIN64 -DCONSERVATIVE -D__USE_MINGW_ANSI_
STDIO -DPERL_TEXTMODE_SCRIPTS -DPERL_IMPLICIT_CONTEXT -DPERL_IMPLICIT_
SYS -DUSE_PERLIO -fwrapv -fno-strict-aliasing -mms-bitfields'
optimize='-s -O2'
cppflags='-DWIN32'
ccversion=''
gccversion='8.3.0'
gccosandvers=''
intsize=4
longsize=4
ptrsize=8
doublesize=8
byteorder=12345678
doublekind=3
d_longlong=define
longlongsize=8
d_longdbl=define
longdblsize=16
longdblkind=3
```

```
    ivtype='long long'
    ivsize=8
    nvtype='double'
    nvsize=8
    Off_t='long long'
    lseeksize=8
    alignbytes=8
    prototype=define
  Linker and Libraries:
    ld='g++'
    ldflags ='-s -L"C:\STRAWB~1\perl\lib\CORE" -L"C:\STRAWB~1\c\lib"'
    libpth=C:\STRAWB~1\c\lib C:\STRAWB~1\c\x86_64-w64-mingw32\lib
    C:\STRAWB~1\c\lib\gcc\x86_64-w64-mingw32\8.3.0
    libs= -lmoldname -lkernel32 -luser32 -lgdi32 -lwinspool -lcomdlg32
    -ladvapi32 -lshell32 -lole32 -loleaut32 -lnetapi32 -luuid -lws2_32
    -lmpr -lwinmm -lversion -lodbc32 -lodbccp32 -lcomctl32
    perllibs= -lmoldname -lkernel32 -luser32 -lgdi32 -lwinspool -lcomdlg32
    -ladvapi32 -lshell32 -lole32 -loleaut32 -lnetapi32 -luuid -lws2_32
    -lmpr -lwinmm -lversion -lodbc32 -lodbccp32 -lcomctl32
    libc=
    so=dll
    useshrplib=true
    libperl=libperl530.a
    gnulibc_version=''
  Dynamic Linking:
    dlsrc=dl_win32.xs
    dlext=xs.dll
    d_dlsymun=undef
    ccdlflags=' '
    cccdlflags=' '
    lddlflags='-mdll -s -L"C:\STRAWB~1\perl\lib\CORE" -L"C:\STRAWB~1\c\lib"'

Characteristics of this binary (from libperl):
  Compile-time options:
    HAS_TIMES
```

```
    HAVE_INTERP_INTERN
    MULTIPLICITY
    PERLIO_LAYERS
    PERL_COPY_ON_WRITE
    PERL_DONT_CREATE_GVSV
    PERL_IMPLICIT_CONTEXT
    PERL_IMPLICIT_SYS
    PERL_MALLOC_WRAP
    PERL_OP_PARENT
    PERL_PRESERVE_IVUV
    USE_64_BIT_INT
    USE_ITHREADS
    USE_LARGE_FILES
    USE_LOCALE
    USE_LOCALE_COLLATE
    USE_LOCALE_CTYPE
    USE_LOCALE_NUMERIC
    USE_LOCALE_TIME
    USE_PERLIO
    USE_PERL_ATOF
  Built under MSWin32
  Compiled at Nov 22 2019 02:30:43
  @INC:
    C:/Strawberry/perl/site/lib
    C:/Strawberry/perl/vendor/lib
    C:/Strawberry/perl/lib
```

Note #1   Most of these values come from the **Config.pm** module. This module was created when Perl was installed on the system. If changes occur on the system (e.g., the C compiler is moved to another directory), you may need to change the **Config.pm** module to reflect this change.

Note #2 ·While it is possible to change the **@INC** array from within the **Config.pm** file, you may want to avoid it. The **@INC** array is derived from preset scalar variables within the **Config.pm** file. You don't normally want to change these variables as they are typically used for other Perl features. It is normally better to have the programmer modify the **@INC** array within their own program.

Extracting scripts from messages

If you have a Perl script that is embedded within a file (such as a "mail file"), then the **-x** option can be very useful. The **-x** option tells Perl to search the file until it finds a line that starts with the string "#!" and also contains the word "perl". It will consider this the first line of code and execute from this line to the bottom of the file.

For example, when run with the **-x** option, the following file (called **embed1.txt**) will display the string "please attend all meetings":

> To: Bob Jones
>
> From: Ted Smith
>
> Date: 2/3/99

Hey Bob,
Please check this code for me!
Thanks,
-Ted

```
#!perl
#embed.pl

print "please attend all meetings\n";
```

Handling extra text after end of script

If there is additional text after the end of the embedded script, you can tell Perl to stop executing code by using the __END__ token (filename **embed2.txt**):

> To: Bob Jones
>
> From: Ted Smith
>
> Date: 2/3/99
>
> Hey Bob,
>
> Please check this code for me!

```perl
#!perl -w
#embed2.pl

use strict;
print "please attend all meetings\n";

__END__
```

> Thanks,
> -Ted

Additional resources

In each chapter, resources are provided to provide the learner with a source for more information. These resources may include downloadable source code or links to other books or articles that will provide you more information about the topic at hand.

Resources for this chapter can be found here:

https://github.com/apress/advanced-perl-programming

Lab exercises

<u>Step #1</u>

Copy the file /etc/skel/local.login into your home directory (note: this file is also in the "examples" directory of the course files on GitHub: https://github.com/advanced-perl-programming). Using the **-p** option, perform the following changes to the file:

1. Replace all digits with dashes (e.g., 123 → ---).

2. Make all capital letters lowercase.

3. Replace all double quotes with single quotes.

<u>Step #2</u>

Have the output of the script replace the original file. Make a backup of the original file called "*file*.old" where *file* is the name of the file that you are modifying.

CHAPTER 2

References

References are a powerful feature of Perl which allow you to perform several advanced operations. For example, to create complex data structures, such as arrays of arrays and hashes of hashes, you need to use references. This chapter will cover what references are as well as how to use references for different advanced operations.

Important note Understanding references is critical to understanding how to make "multi-dimensional arrays", "multi-dimensional hashes", object-oriented Perl programs, as well as other advanced Perl features. This chapter focuses primarily on how to create and use references; functional uses of references will be covered in later chapters.

When a scalar variable is assigned a value, this process is called assignment by value. For example, the following two commands demonstrate assignment by value:

```
$c=5;
$d=$c;
```

Conceptually, Perl will store the value of the variables like this:

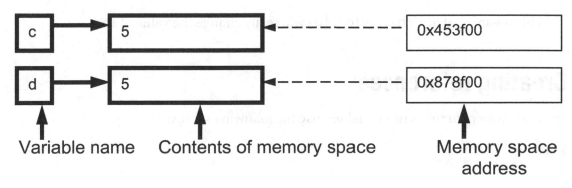

Variable name   Contents of memory space   Memory space address

© William "Bo" Rothwell of One Course Source, Inc. 2020
W. "Bo" Rothwell, *Advanced Perl Programming*, https://doi.org/10.1007/978-1-4842-5863-7_2

Note   The "0x453f00" and "0x787f00" represent the memory address where the values of the variables are stored.

A reference is a **scalar value** that refers to another scalar value (or array, associative array, function, etc.). An example of when variables are assigned by reference is when values are passed into a function as arguments:

```
sub total {return ($_[0] * $_[1];}
$c=5;
$d=4;
print &total($c, $d);
```

Conceptually, Perl will store the value of the variables like this:

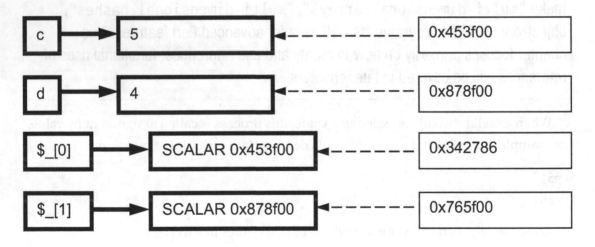

This means that any changes to $_[0] will really change the value of $a.

Creating references

To create your own reference variables, use the following syntax:

```
$var1 = \$var2;
```

Example:

```
DB<1> $name="Bob"
DB<2> $person = \$name
```

You can also make reference variables to arrays and associative arrays (and other types that we will see later):

```
$var1=\@array;
$var2=\%hash;
```

Note   Reference variables are always scalar variables regardless of what they refer to. This is because the value that is assigned to the variable (called the *referent*) is always a scalar value.

Returning the value from a reference

Once you have created a reference variable, you can't treat it exactly like a regular scalar variable. If you do, you won't get the value that the reference variable pointed to:

```
DB<1> $name="Bob"
DB<2> @colors=qw(red green blue)
DB<3> %cities=("San Diego" => "CA", "Boston" => "MA", "Denver" => "CO")
DB<4> $person=\$name
DB<5> $hue=\@colors
DB<6> $town=\%cities
DB<7> print $person
SCALAR(0x1e07b0)
DB<8> print $hue
ARRAY(0x1a1864)
DB<9> print $town
HASH(0x1a1918)
```

21

The return value that you are seeing in the preceding examples [SCALAR(0x1e07b0), for example] is called a *referent*. The referent is what Perl uses to refer to the original variable. It contains the type of the referent (e.g., SCALAR) and the memory location of what it is referring to (e.g., 0x1e07b0).

In order to return a scalar value that the reference is "pointing to", you can use the **$$** notation:

```
DB<1> $name="Bob"
DB<2> @colors=qw(red green blue)
DB<3> %cities=("San Diego" => "CA", "Boston" => "MA", "Denver" => "CO")
DB<4> $person=\$name
DB<5> $hue=\@colors
DB<6> $town=\%cities
DB<7> print $$person
Bob
DB<8> print $$hue[0]
red
DB<9> print $$town{Boston}
MA
```

It's important that you use the **$$** notation and not use just one dollar sign character. Consider the following examples:

```
DB<1> $name=Bob;
DB<2> $person=\$name;
DB<3> $$person="Ted";        #changes $name
DB<4> $person="Sue";         #breaks the reference
```

Other methods of referencing arrays

You can use two additional methods to use a reference to an array:

```
DB<1> @colors=qw(red green blue)
DB<2> $hue=\@colors
DB<3> print $hue->[0]
red
DB<4> print ${$hue}[0]
red
```

The second method isn't much different than just using $$hue[0] method as the curly braces are just used for clarity. This method is typically used when accessing the entire array

```
DB<1> @colors=qw(red green blue)
DB<2> $hue=\@colors
DB<3> print @{$hue}
red green blue
```

or when using the "last index position" variable:

```
DB<1> @colors=qw(red green blue)
DB<2> $hue=\@colors
DB<3> print $#{$hue}
2
```

In both these cases, the curly braces are not required.

If you want to loop through all of the elements in an array that is being accessed via a reference, you can use the following syntax:

```
DB<1> @colors=qw(red green blue)
DB<2> $hue=\@colors
DB<3> foreach $element (@{$hue}) {print "$element\n";}
red
green
blue
```

But, in *almost* all cases, the curly braces are not needed. They just make it more clear to someone reading the program that **$hue** is a reference.

Arrays of scalar references

Note that the preceding method is different than if you used "${$hue[0]}". This method tells Perl to return the array scalar value $hue[0] as a reference. This can be useful if you want to have an array of references:

```
DB<1> $name1="Bob"
DB<2> $name2="Ted"
DB<3> $name3="Sue"
```

```
DB<4> @people=(\$name1, \$name2, \$name3)
DB<5> print ${$people[0]}
Bob
```

Note: Line #4 could also be written as

```
@people=\($name1, $name2, $name2);
```

Another method of referencing hashes

Another method that you can use for references to hashes is

```
DB<1> %cities=("San Diego" => "CA", "Boston" => "MA", "Denver" => "CO")
DB<2> $town=\%cities
DB<3> print $town->{"San Diego"}
CA
```

Note   The syntax `${$town}{"San Diego"}` will also work.

The ref function

The **ref** function will return a string that describes the type of reference:

```
DB<1> $name="Bob"
DB<2> @colors=qw(red green blue)
DB<3> %cities=("San Diego" => "CA", "Boston" => "MA", "Denver" => "CO")
DB<4> $person=\$name
DB<5> $hue=\@colors
DB<6> $town=\%cities
DB<7> print ref $person
SCALAR
DB<8> print ref $hue
ARRAY
DB<9> print ref $town
HASH
```

If the variable isn't a reference, then the **ref** function will return a null string. This allows you to use the return value of **ref** as a conditional statement:

```
if (ref $var) {
    print "It's a reference";
}
else
{
    print "It's not a reference";
}
```

The **ref** function can return one of the following values:

SCALAR	Reference to a scalar variable
ARRAY	Reference to an array variable
HASH	Reference to an associative array variable
CODE	Reference to a procedure
REF	Reference to a reference
GLOB	Reference to a typeglob (typeglobs are discussed in a future Unit)

Making anonymous references

You don't have to specify an existing array or hash to make a reference variable to an array or hash. You can make a reference variable to an *anonymous* array or hash.

To create a reference to an anonymous array, you can use one of two techniques.

Method #1

```
$arrayref=[ "bob", "sue", "ted" ];
```

In this example, Perl is explicitly told that the list of names is an anonymous array as a result of the square brackets around the list.

Method #2

```
@$arrayref=("bob", "sue", "ted");
```

In this example, you are specifying that you want to create a reference to an array by using the "@$" notation. Therefore, Perl makes the list of names into an anonymous array because you are assigning the list of names to a reference variable. In other words, you imply that Perl should make a reference to an anonymous array.

Using similar techniques to those shown on the previous page, you can create references to anonymous hashes.

Method #1

```
$hashref={"San Diego" => "CA", "Boston" => "MA", "Denver" => "CO"};
```

Method #2

```
%$hashref=("San Diego" => "CA", "Boston" => "MA", "Denver" => "CO");
```

Note   Once you have created a reference variable to an anonymous array or hash, you can use the reference variable just like if you created a reference variable to an existing array or hash. The only difference between the two is the manner in which you create the reference variable: one method uses data from an existing variable, the other generates the data structure "on the fly".

In a later Unit, we will talk about arrays of arrays and hashes of hashes and see the primary advantage of having anonymous arrays and hashes.

References to functions

You can create a reference to a function as well:

```
DB<1> sub total {print "The total is ", $_[0] * $_[1], "\n";}
DB<2> $result=\&total
DB<3> &$result(4,5)
```

The total is 20
DB<4> **$result -> (4,5)**
The total is 20

The best example of why you would want to create a reference to a function is the
%SIG hash. The **%SIG** hash handles signals that are sent to your program. If you want to
change the default behavior of your script when it received signals, you can modify the
%SIG hash:

```perl
#!perl
sleep1.pl

sub nostop {
    print "Can't stop this!\n";
}

$SIG{INT}=\&nostop;     #Ignore control-c

print "countdown!\n\n";
$|=1;
for ($i=10;$i>0;$i--) {
    print "$i \r";
    sleep 1;
}
$|=0;
print "Blast off!\n";
```

You want to assign the key "INT" to a reference to the &nostop function in a situation
like this. If you assigned it to the &nostop function directly, the function would be run
prior to the assignment operation and the return value of the function would be assigned
to the key "INT".

You can also create references to anonymous functions:

```perl
#!perl
#sleep2.pl

$SIG{INT}=sub {print "Can't stop this!\n"}; #Ignore control-c
```

27

```
print "countdown!\n\n";
$|=1;
for ($i=10;$i>0;$i--) {
    print "$i \r";
    sleep 1;
}
$|=0;
print "Blast off!\n";
```

use strict 'refs'

Suppose you execute the following two statements:

```
DB<1> $name="Bob"
DB<2> $$name="Ted"
```

In this example, you ask Perl to assign the value "Ted" to the variable that the scalar variable $name refers to. However, $name doesn't refer to anything... it is set to a scalar value "Bob".

In this case, like many in Perl, Perl tries to make due with the information that you provided and generate the most reasonable result. The result: Perl creates a scalar variable called $Bob that is assigned the value "Ted":

```
DB<1> $name="Bob"
DB<2> $$name="Ted"
DB<3> print $Bob
Ted
```

This process is called "symbolic references". The methods we used in the previous sections are called "hard references".

Typically, you want to avoid symbolic references. Not only are they confusing, but they can cause additional problems. It is easy to accidentally make a symbolic reference when you really intended to make a hard reference.

To avoid making symbolic references by accident, use the **use strict 'refs'** statement:

```
#!perl
#strict.pl
```

```
use strict 'refs';

$name="Bob";
$$name="Ted";
```

Example output of strict.pl:

```
[student@linux1 student]$ ./strict.pl
Can't use string ("Bob") as a SCALAR ref while "strict refs" in use at ./
strict.pl line 7.
```

Note   You can allow symbolic references later in your script by using the following statement:

```
no strict 'refs';
```

Making use of symbolic references

You may be wondering why symbolic references are permitted in the first place. For example, suppose you want to keep track of the average rainfall per month in San Diego. Because the months are in order, you choose to use an array rather than a hash to store these values:

```
@rain=(1.1, 0.9, 0.8, 0.4, 0, 0, 0, 0.2, 2.0, 1,8, 0.9, 1.2);
```

The first value in the array represents the rainfall in January, the second value represents February, and so on. So, to display the rainfall for March, you could execute the following:

```
print $rain[2];
```

However, this is a bit unnatural because most people consider March to be the third month in the year. You could overcome this by introducing a dummy value as the first element in the array:

```
@rain=(undef, 1.1, 0.9, 0.8, 0.4, 0, 0, 0, 0.2, 2.0, 1,8, 0.9, 1.2);
```

However, this is also unnatural as there is now a undefined element in the array. You could also use a hash instead, but you would lose the "order" feature that arrays provide. It would be nice if you could use a month name instead of an index value… and you can with symbolic references.

To start, create regular variables as follows:

```
$JANUARY      = 0;
$FEBRUARY     = 1;
$MARCH        = 2;
$APRIL        = 3;
$MAY          = 4;
$JUNE         = 5;
$JULY         = 6;
$AUGUST       = 7;
$SEPTEMBER    = 8;
$OCTOBER      = 9;
$NOVEMBER     = 10;
$DECEMBER     = 11;
```

Now you can use the variable name to look up a value:

```
DB<1> $MARCH=3
DB<2> @rain=(1.1, 0.9, 0.8, 0.4, 0, 0, 0, 0.2, 2.0, 1,8, 0.9, 1.2);
DB<3> print $rain[$MARCH]
0.4
```

Of course, this isn't symbolic references (yet). To consider why you would want to use, consider the following code:

```
DB<1> $MARCH=3;
DB<2> @rain=(1.1, 0.9, 0.8, 0.4, 0, 0, 0, 0.2, 2.0, 1,8, 0.9, 1.2);
DB<3> print "Enter a month to print: "; $month=<STDIN>
Enter a month to print: MARCH
DB<4> chomp $month
```

Now the variable $month contains the value of MARCH. If you try to use this variable as shown in the following, the wrong result will be returned:

```
DB<5> print $rain[$month]
1.1
```

The value within the [ ] must be a numeric value. When the value of $month is returned (MARCH), it is converted into the number 0. However, by using a symbolic reference, the variable $MARCH can return the value of 2 and the correct result will be displayed:

```
DB<6> print $rain[$$month]
0.4
```

Now you have an array that has a very flexible indexing method: by numeric value (0, 1, 2, etc.), by name ($JANUARY, $FEBRUARY, $MARCH, etc.), or by name provided by user input ($$input).

Additional resources

In each chapter, resources are provided to provide the learner with a source for more information. These resources may include downloadable source code or links to other books or articles that will provide you more information about the topic at hand.

Resources for this chapter can be found here:

```
https://github.com/apress/advanced-perl-programming
```

Lab exercises

No exercises for this lab.

CHAPTER 3

Advanced Data Types: Arrays

Knowing references (see Chapter 2) allows you to perform some advanced coding in Perl, including making arrays of arrays (a.k.a. multi-dimensional arrays). This chapter introduces this topic as well as some other advanced features of arrays.

What you should already know about arrays

Note In the *Beginning Perl Programming* and *Pro Perl Programming* books, we covered some of the basics of arrays. This section is meant to be a review of these topics.

Array variables are used to store lists (groups) of scalar data. Important general information about array variables:

- The variable starts with a "@" symbol (not a $ symbol like scalar variables).

- The variable name must start with either an alpha character or underscore character and only can consist of alphanumeric and underscore character.

- Array sizes don't have to be declared; Perl takes care of the size of the array dynamically.

- Individual scalar data within the array are referred to as "elements".

- An element can be a string or number.

© William "Bo" Rothwell of One Course Source, Inc. 2020
W. "Bo" Rothwell, *Advanced Perl Programming*, https://doi.org/10.1007/978-1-4842-5863-7_3

Creating arrays

To create an array, use the following syntax:

```
@names=("Bob", "Sue", "Ted");
```

Returning values in arrays

To return the value of an element in an array, use the following syntax:

```
print "$names[0] is the first name in the list\n";
```

    Array elements are indexed by integers (starting from 0). Therefore, the first element is element "0", the second element is element "1", and so forth.

    To print the last element of an array:

```
print "$names[$#names] \n";
#or:
print "$names[-1] \n";
```

    To print the entire array:

```
print "@names";
```

Note   Without the quotes (" "), all of the elements would be printed "mashed together".

Adding and removing elements in an array

You can use built-in functions to add and remove elements in an array. The built-in functions are as follows:

Push	**Add new element to end of array**
Unshift	**Add new element to beginning of array**
Pop	**Remove (and return) last element of array**
Shift	**Remove (and return) first element of array**
Splice	**Add or remove element(s) in any position in the array**

To manually add elements in an array, assign the array to "itself" **and** the elements you wish to add:

```
@flowers=(@flowers, "daisy");         #puts daisy at end of array.


@flowers=("carnation", @flowers);    #puts carnation at beginning of array.
```

To manually remove elements in an array, assign the array **and** a scalar variable to the array itself:

```
($plant, @flowers)=@flowers;          #Assigns @flowers to all but the first
                                      #element which is placed in $plant.
```

Looping through the array

There are two commonly used techniques to loop through an array in Perl. The first technique is using a for loop.

In the following example, the **for** loop will print out each element of an array on a separate line:

```
@arr=("north", "south", "east", "west");
for ($i=0; $i <= $#arr; $i++) {
   print "$arr[$i]\n";
}
```

The second technique is to use a **foreach** loop. The following code will print out each element of an array (like the previous example) using the **foreach** loop:

```
@arr=("north", "south", "east", "west");
foreach $direction (@arr) {
   print "$direction\n";
}
```

Important note: The name of the array **must** be within parentheses () in a **foreach** loop.

Array operators

There are a few operators that assist you in manipulating arrays.

The reverse operator

The **reverse** operator will return the reverse of an array:

```
@arr=("north", "south", "east", "west");
@revarr = reverse (@arr);
print "@revarr";                    #prints west east south north
```

The sort operator

The **sort** operator will perform an ASCII sort of the elements of an array:

```
@arr=("north", "south", "east", "west");
@sortarr = sort (@arr);
print "@sortarr";                   #prints "east north south west"
```

There are other "types" of sorts that you can perform; for example, the following performs a numeric sort:

```
@num=(10,7,99,93,0);
@sortnum=sort {$a <=> $b} (@num);
print "@sortnum";                   #prints 0 7 10 93 99
```

The qw operator

The **qw** (quote words) operator will create a comma, quoted separated list from its arguments. It is primarily used as a shorthand method of creating lists. For example, the following array declaration

```
@directions= ('n', 's', 'e', 'w', 'ne', 'nw', 'se', 'sw');
```

can be rewritten using **qw** like this:

```
@directions=qw(n s e w ne nw se sw);
```

For a double quoted string, use the qq( ) function.

Array separator variable

When you print an array, all of the elements of the array are displayed "merged together":

```
DB<1> @colors=qw(red blue green purple)
DB<2> print @colors
redbluegreenpurple
```

When you place quotes around the array, each element is separated with a space:

```
DB<1> @colors=qw(red blue green purple)
DB<2> print "@colors"
red blue green purple
```

The **$"** variable stores what character(s) should be used to separate array elements when the array name is placed within quotes. By default, this variable is set to a space. To change this behavior, just set the variable to a different character:

```
DB<1> @colors=qw(red blue green purple)
DB<2> $"=":"
DB<3> print "@colors"
red:blue:green:purple
```

Regular expression matching with grep

While regular expressions pattern matching works well with strings, it's a bit of a pain for elements in an array. The **grep** statement will look at each element of an array and return those that match the expression:

```
#!/usr/bin/perl
#grep.pl

@array=qw(Bob Bobby Ted Fred Sue Nick Sally);
@b=grep (/^B/, @array);
print "@b";
```

What you might know about arrays

Based on your experiences with Perl, you may have learned some of the following features and techniques of working with arrays. While not all of the following topics are "advanced", any advanced Perl programmer should be aware of them.

Changing $#array changes the size of the array

You can truncate an array or add "empty" elements to an array by changing the size of "$#array" (where "array" is replaced by the name of the array):

```
DB<1> @colors=qw(red blue yellow green purple white tan)
DB<2> x @colors
0   'red'
1   'blue'
2   'yellow'
3   'green'
4   'purple'
5   'white'
6   'tan'
DB<3> print $#colors
6
DB<4> $#colors=3

DB<5> x @colors
0   'red'
1   'blue'
2   'yellow'
3   'green'
DB<6> $#colors=7
DB<7> x @colors
0   'red'
1   'blue'
2   'yellow
3   'green'
4   undef
```

```
5   undef
6   undef
7   undef
```

Arrays returned in scalar context returns the number of elements in the array

When you use an array in a scalar situation, it is called "returning an array in scalar context". Instead of returning all of the elements in the array, Perl returns the number of elements in the array:

```
DB<1> @colors=qw(red blue green)
DB<2> $result=@colors
DB<3> print $result
3
```

You can also explicitly have Perl return the scalar context of an array by using the **scalar** statement:

```
DB<1> @colors=qw(red blue green)
DB<2> $result=scalar @colors
DB<3> print $result
3
```

This can be useful when you want the scalar value of an array in a situation in which Perl wouldn't return the scalar context naturally.

Changing the variable in a foreach loop changes the array elements

While executing a **foreach** loop, if you modify the "foreach variable", you will modify the value in the array. This is because the "foreach variable" is a reference to the element in the array. Example:

```
DB<1> @colors=qw(red blue yellow green)
DB<2> foreach $name (@colors) {\
  cont:      if ($name =~ /^b/) {\
```

```
    cont:              $name="null"; }}
DB<3> print "@colors"
red null yellow green
```

The $_ variable is used by default in a foreach loop

This is a handy, often used trick among advanced Perl programmers. The following code

```
foreach $col (@colors) {
    print "found red!\n" if ($col =~ m/red/);
}
```

could be written like this instead:

```
foreach (@colors) {
    print "found red!\n" if /red/;
}
```

This is also an easy, useful way to "replace" a traditional (and bulky) **for** loop:

```
foreach (1..10) {
    print "$_\n";
}
```

The foreach loop and for loops are the same thing

Technically, the **foreach** loop is just a synonym for the **for** loop, which means that this code

```
foreach $var (@array) {
    print "$var\n";
}
```

is the same as this code:

```
for $var (@array) {
    print "$var\n";
}
```

And this code

```
for ($i=1; $i <= 10; $i++) {
   print "$i\n";
}
```

is the same as this code:

```
foreach ($i=1; $i <= 10; $i++) {
   print "$i\n";
}
```

Arrays of arrays

Arrays are excellent for keeping track of lists of items. However, suppose you need to keep track of not only a list of items but a corresponding list for each of those items.

For example, suppose you want to keep track of transactions of your bank account. In order to do this, you need to keep track of four bits of data per transaction:

1. Type of transaction

2. Date of transaction

3. Comment for the transaction

4. Amount of transaction

Example data:

Transaction type	Date	Comment	Amount
DEP	12/12/1999	Beginning Balance	1000
DEP	12/13/1999	Payday!	500
WD	12/14/1999	Rent check (#101)	400
WD	12/15/1999	Cash	100

There are a few approaches that we can use to keep track of this information.

Method #1 – Make an array for each data type

```
@trans=qw(DEP DEP WD WD);
@date=qw(12/12/1999 12/13/1999 12/14/1999 12/15/1999);
@comment=("Beginning Balance", "Payday!", "Rent check (#101)", "Cash");
@amount=(1000, 500, 400, 100);
```

This method is very difficult to work with.

Method #2 – Make an array for each transaction

```
@trans1=("DEP", "12/12/1999" , "Beginning Balance", "1000");
@trans2=("DEP", "12/13/1999" , "Payday!", "500");
@trans3=("WD", "12/14/1999" , "Rent check (#101)", "400");
@trans4=("WD", "12/15/1999" , "Cash", "100");
```

Once again, although this will work, it's difficult to work with.

Method #3 – Make an array of arrays

The best method is to make an array whose values are themselves arrays. This is often referred to as a multi-dimensional array.

Creating arrays of arrays

To create an array of arrays, use the following syntax:

```
@trans = (
    ["DEP", "12/12/1999" , "Beginning Balance", "1000"],
    ["DEP", "12/13/1999" , "Payday!", "500"],
    ["WD", "12/14/1999" , "Rent check (#101)", "400"],
    ["WD", "12/15/1999" , "Cash", "100"]);
```

The preceding example creates four **references** to four **anonymous arrays**.

For example, the first value of the @trans array is the array that contains the values "DEP", "12/12/1999", "Beginning Balance", and "1000".

The term array can cause some confusion from this point on. For that reason, the top-most array (@trans in the preceding example) will be called "the array", and the "inner" arrays will be referred to as "subarrays" or "row" (see next paragraph) for the rest of this Unit.

Rows and columns

The best way to think about how the data is being arranged is in terms of rows and columns. A row in this case is a subarray. A column is all of the "like" values from each subarray.

Creating a multi-dimensional array from STDIN

You can read data from STDIN and add it to a multi-dimensional array using the following technique

```
while (<STDIN>) {
    @temp = split;
    push (@trans, [@temp]);
}
```

or to avoid the unnecessary @temp variable

```
while (<STDIN>) {
    push (@trans, [ split ]);
}
```

Example:

```
#!perl
#3_create.pl

print "Enter transaction (sep items by a space): ";

while (<STDIN>) {
    push (@trans, [split]);
}
```

Accessing values in an array of arrays

Once you have created an array of an array, you can access a scalar value of a subarray by using the following syntax:

```perl
#!perl
#aoa.pl

@trans = (
    ["DEP", "12/12/1999", "Beginning Balance", "1000"],
    ["DEP", "12/13/1999", "Payday!",           "500"],
    ["WD",  "12/14/1999", "Rent Check (#101)", "400"],
    ["WD",  "12/15/1999", "Cash",              "100"]);

print "$trans[0][2]\n";  #prints "Beginning Balance";
```

Adding a subarray (row)

The example in Creating arrays of arrays showed how to create the array. To add a subarray, use the following syntax:

```perl
@temp=("DEP", "12/18/1999", "Found some money", "200");
push (@trans, [@temp]);
```

Note   It is very important to place the square brackets around the subarray. If you don't, the return value of the subarray won't be an array; it will be the scalar value of the array (the number of items in the array). Remember, the square brackets indicate to Perl that you want to create a reference to an anonymous array.

Adding a column

Suppose you want to add an additional bit of data to each subarray. For example, suppose we want to add a "cleared" field for each subarray in our @trans array.

This field will be used to indicate if the transaction has cleared the bank or not. If this field is set to 0, then the transaction hasn't cleared the bank yet. If this field is set to 1, then the transaction has cleared.

In order to do this, we can use the following:

```perl
for ($i=0 ; $i <= $#trans; $i++) {
    print "Has the \"$trans[$i][2]\" transaction cleared (1=yes, 0=no)? ";
    chomp($c=<STDIN>);
    $trans[$i][4]=$c;
}
```

Printing an array of arrays

If you just want to print one element of a subarray, then the technique is easy:

```perl
print $trans[x][y];
```

If you want to print all of the elements of each subarray, then it can get a little tricky.
Here is one method:

```perl
#!perl
#print1.pl

@trans = (
    ["DEP", "12/12/1999", "Beginning Balance", "1000"],
    ["DEP", "12/13/1999", "Payday!",           "500"],
    ["WD",  "12/14/1999", "Rent Check (#101)", "400"],
    ["WD",  "12/15/1999", "Cash",              "100"]);

for ($i=0; $i <= $#trans; $i++) {
    print "Type: $trans[$i][0]\n";
    print "Date: $trans[$i][1]\n";
    print "Comment: $trans[$i][2]\n";
    print "Amount: $trans[$i][3]\n";
    print "\n";
}
```

The method on the preceding page works well if you know how many columns there are. If you don't know how many columns there are, you will need to determine this by using references:

```perl
#!perl
#print2.pl

@trans = (
    ["DEP", "12/12/1999", "Beginning Balance", "1000", 1],
    ["DEP", "12/13/1999", "Payday!",              "500"],
    ["WD",  "12/14/1999", "Rent Check (#101)"],
    ["WD",  "12/15/1999", "Cash",                 "100"]);

foreach $row (@trans) {
    foreach $col (@$row) {
        print "$col\t";
    }
    print "\n";
}

#or:
#for ($i=0; $i <= $#trans; $i++) {
#    for ($j=0; $j <= $#{$trans[$i]}; $j++) {
#        print "$trans[$i][$j]\t";
#    }
#    print "\n";
#}
```

Output of print2.pl:

```
[student@linux1 student]$ print2.pl
DEP     12/12/1999      Beginning Balance       1000    1
DEP     12/13/1999      Payday! 500
WD      12/14/1999      Rent Check (#101)
WD      12/15/1999      Cash    100
```

Additional resources

In each chapter, resources are provided to provide the learner with a source for more information. These resources may include downloadable source code or links to other books or articles that will provide you more information about the topic at hand.

Resources for this chapter can be found here:

`https://github.com/apress/advanced-perl-programming`

Lab exercises

Step #1

Create a script that uses arrays of arrays to keep track of a database of `"open tickets"`. An open ticket in this case is a complaint by a customer that hasn't yet been resolved. The operator of this script will have the following options:

1. List all open tickets

2. Add a ticket item

3. Delete a ticket item

4. List all complaints

5. Exit the script

Notes:

*   Each element of the array will contain a subarray that will have three elements: Date the ticket was opened, Customer name, and `"complaint"`.

*   Use a `"global"` variable to store the data in this `"array of arrays"`.

*   Use a format statement to make option #1 `"look nice"`.

Step #2

Make the following improvements to your script:

1. Have the data saved into a file when the script ends.

2. Have the data read from your file into the array when the script begins.

CHAPTER 4

Advanced Data Types: Hashes

Knowing references (see Chapter 2) allows you to perform some advanced coding in Perl, including making hashes of hashes (a.k.a. multi-dimensional hashes). This chapter introduces this topic as well as some other advanced features of hashes.

What you should already know about hashes

Note   In the *Beginning Perl Programming* and *Pro Perl Programming* books, we covered some of the basics of hashes. This section is meant to be a review of these topics.

Hashes are useful when you need to store data that is related to (or associated with) other data, for example, if we want to keep a list of dog names and their owners' names as well.

Notes about associative arrays:

- Associative arrays are also called `"hashes"`.

- Associative array variables start with a percent sign (%).

- The term index is used for regular arrays; the term "key" is used for associative arrays.

- The key/value pair is stored in a seemingly `"random"` order.
  Note the comment about this in the perlsec documentation guide
  (`http://perldoc.perl.org/perlsec.html#Algorithmic-Complexity-Attacks`):

© William "Bo" Rothwell of One Course Source, Inc. 2020
W. "Bo" Rothwell, *Advanced Perl Programming*, https://doi.org/10.1007/978-1-4842-5863-7_4

Hash Algorithm - Hash algorithms like the one used in Perl are well known to be vulnerable to collision attacks on their hash function. Such attacks involve constructing a set of keys which collide into the same bucket producing inefficient behavior. Such attacks often depend on discovering the seed of the hash function used to map the keys to buckets. That seed is then used to brute-force a key set which can be used to mount a denial of service attack. In Perl 5.8.1 changes were introduced to harden Perl to such attacks, and then later in Perl 5.18.0 these features were enhanced and additional protections added.

Creating associative arrays

There are two different (syntax) methods of creating an associative array:

```
%dog_owners=qw(Bob Fido Sue Spot Fred Teddy Sally Rex);

%dog_owners=(
    Bob=>    Fido,
    Sue=>    Spot,
    Fred=>   Teddy,
    Sally=>  Rex
);
```

To create an individual key/value pair, use the following syntax:

```
$dog_owners{Nick}="Mikey";
```

Accessing values in an associative array

To access a value of a key, use the following syntax:

```
print "$dog_owners{Bob} is owned by Bob\n";
```

There are two method of "looping" (accessing every key/value pair separately) though associative arrays: using a **foreach** loop or using a "**while-each**" loop. Each method has its advantage and disadvantage.

The **keys** function will return all of the keys of an associative array. These keys are returned in a list format and can either be assigned to an array or manipulated like an array:

```
@owners=keys (%dog_owners);
print "@owners";
foreach $person (keys %dog_owners) {
   print "$dog_owners{$person} is owned by $person\n";
}
```

The disadvantage of the **foreach** method is that a second (regular) array is created when the **keys** statement is used. This is a disadvantage because it takes more memory to store this extra array and it takes time to create the extra array.

A **"while-each"** loop doesn't create an extra array. Instead, it extracts key/value pairs one at a time and assigns them to scalar variables:

```
while (($key, $value) = each (%dog_owners)) {
   print "$value is owned by $key\n";
}
```

The biggest disadvantage with a "while-each" loop is what takes place when the associative array is modified within the loop. Any modification of the associative array (adding key/value pairs, removing key/value pairs, or changing existing key/value pairs) can cause a "rehash".

This rehash is a reorganization of how the array is stored in memory. If a rehash occurs, the "while-each" loop will "start over".

Note from http://perldoc.perl.org/functions/each.html: "In the current implementation, it is always safe to delete the item most recently returned by each()".

The **values** function can be used to access just the values of the key/value pair:

```
@dogs=values (%dog_owners);
```

This can be useful if you want to find out how many dogs are named "Spot":

```
foreach $name (values (%dog_owners)) {
   if ($name eq "Spot") {
      $spot++;
   }
}
```

Removing associative array keys and values

To remove both the key and value of an associative array, use the **delete** statement:

```
delete $dog_owners{Bob};
```

To remove the value, but keep the key, use the **undef** statement:

```
undef $dog_owners{Fred};
```

exists vs. defined

The **defined** statement can also be used to determine if a value of a key/value pair has been defined:

```
if (defined ($dog_owners{Nick})) {
    print "Nick has a dog\n";
}
else
{
    print "Nick doesn't have a dog\n";
}
```

While the **defined** statement is used to determine if the value has been set, the **exists** statement is used to determine if the *key* exists:

```
%dog_owners=(Bob, Fido, Sue, Spot, Fred, Teddy, Sally, Rex);
undef $dog_owners{Bob};
if (defined ($dog_owners{Bob}) {      #false in this case
    print "Bob has a dog\n";
} else {
    print "Bob doesn't have a dog\n";
}
if (exists ($dog_owners{Bob}) {       #true in this case
    print "Bob is a key in the array\n";
} else {
    print "Bob is not a key in the array\n";
}
```

What you might know about hashes
Keeping order in hashes

Since hashes store key/value pairs, the order that the data is stored isn't so important. However, suppose the order of hashes was important and you want the order to be the same as how you created the hash. In this case, use the module Tie::IxHash.

When you use Tie::IxHash on a hash, it tells **keys**, **values**, and **each** to return the hash elements in the same order in which they were created:

```
#!perl
#order.pl

use Tie::IxHash;
tie %data, "Tie::IxHash";

%data=qw(bob 1-800-898-5555 ted 1-888-989-5555 sue 1-619-469-5555);

@keys=keys (%data);
print "@keys", "\n";
```

The following output demonstrates order.pl when the "use Tie::IxHash"; statement is commented out. Note that the order of the keys as they are returned is not the original order that the keys were in when the hash was created:

```
[student@OCS student]$ perl order.pl
sue bob ted
```

In the following example, the "use Tie::IxHash"; statement is not commented out and the order of the keys is consistent with the original order when the hash was created:

```
C:\ >perl order.pl
bob ted sue
```

Important note   The Tie::IxHash module is not part of the default Perl installation. You may need to install this module (Chapter 9 for information on installing Perl modules). The following provides an example of one method you could use to install this module (executed on a Windows system using Strawberry Perl).

```
C:\>cpan
Loading internal logger. Log::Log4perl recommended for better logging

    Unable to get Terminal Size. The Win32 GetConsoleScreenBufferInfo call
didn't work. The COLUMNS and LINES environment variables didn't work. at
C:\Strawberry\perl\vendor\lib/Term/ReadLine/readline.pm line 410.

cpan shell -- CPAN exploration and modules installation (v2.27)
Enter 'h' for help.
cpan> install Tie::IxHash
Fetching with LWP:
http://cpan.strawberryperl.com/authors/01mailrc.txt.gz
Fetching with LWP:
http://cpan.strawberryperl.com/modules/02packages.details.txt.gz
Fetching with LWP:
http://cpan.strawberryperl.com/modules/03modlist.data.gz
Creating database file ... Done!
Running install for module 'Tie::IxHash'
Fetching with LWP:
http://cpan.strawberryperl.com/authors/id/C/CH/CHORNY/Tie-IxHash-1.23.tar.gz
Fetching with LWP:
http://cpan.strawberryperl.com/authors/id/C/CH/CHORNY/CHECKSUMS
Checksum for C:\STRAWB~1\cpan\sources\authors\id\C\CH\CHORNY\Tie-
IxHash-1.23.tar.gz ok
Scanning cache C:\STRAWB~1\cpan\build for sizes
DONE
Configuring C/CH/CHORNY/Tie-IxHash-1.23.tar.gz with Build.PL
Created MYMETA.yml and MYMETA.json
Creating new 'Build' script for 'Tie-IxHash' version '1.23'
  CHORNY/Tie-IxHash-1.23.tar.gz
  C:\Strawberry\perl\bin\perl.exe Build.PL -- OK
Running Build for C/CH/CHORNY/Tie-IxHash-1.23.tar.gz
Building Tie-IxHash
  CHORNY/Tie-IxHash-1.23.tar.gz
  C:\Strawberry\perl\bin\perl.exe ./Build -- OK
Running Build test for CHORNY/Tie-IxHash-1.23.tar.gz
```

```
t\each-delete.t .. ok
t\ixhash.t ....... ok
t\pod.t .......... ok
All tests successful.
Files=3, Tests=29,  1 wallclock secs ( 0.06 usr +  0.00 sys =  0.06 CPU)
Result: PASS
Lockfile removed.
  CHORNY/Tie-IxHash-1.23.tar.gz
  C:\Strawberry\perl\bin\perl.exe ./Build test -- OK
Running Build install for CHORNY/Tie-IxHash-1.23.tar.gz
Building Tie-IxHash
Installing C:\STRAWB~1\perl\site\lib\Tie\IxHash.pm
  CHORNY/Tie-IxHash-1.23.tar.gz
  C:\Strawberry\perl\bin\perl.exe ./Build install --uninst 1 -- OK

cpan> quit
Lockfile removed.

C:\>
```

Additional useful hash modules

In addition to Tie::IxHash, the following modules are useful when using hashes:

Module	Description
Tie::Hash::Sorted	Has **keys**, **values**, and **each** to return the hash elements in sorted order. Can be based on either the key or the value
Tie::Hash::Indexed	Provides the same features as Tie::IxHash, but is potentially faster. May not be available on older versions of Perl
Tie::Hash::MultiValue	Allows you to easily store multiple values per key

As with Tie::IxHash, these modules are not part of a default Perl installation.

Inverting a hash: method #1

There may a time in which you want to make all of your keys into values and vice versa. To do this, you can use the **reverse** statement:

```
#!perl
#rev1.pl

%data=qw(bob 1-800-898-5555 ted 1-888-989-5555 sue 1-619-469-5555);

%numbers=reverse (%data);

print "The phone number 1-888-989-5555 belongs to $numbers{'1-888-989--
5555'}\n";
```

The following demonstrates the output of rev1.pl:

```
[student@OCS student]$ perl rev1.pl

    The phone number 1-888-989-5555 belongs to ted
```

Important note   If you have two or more values that are identical, only the "first" value discovered in the hash will be made into a key. Since the order of the hash is not naturally the order that you created the key/value pairs, the first value discovered in the hash will be "random". As a result, if it is possible to have duplicate values in the hash, consider using the method described on the following page.

Inverting a hash: method #2

The following example handles one of the disadvantages of using the technique described in the previous section. In this example, each value is inspected to determine if it has already been used as a key. If it has not, then a new key/value pair is created in the new "reversed" hash. If the value has been used as a key in the new hash, then data is appended, not overwritten:

```perl
#!perl
#rev2pl

%data=qw(bob 1-888-989-5555 ted 1-888-989-5555 sue 1-619-469-5555);

while (($key, $value) = each (%data)) {
   if (exists ($numbers{$value})) {
      $numbers{$value} .= ":$key";
}
   else {
      $numbers{$value}="$key";
}
}

print "The phone number 1-888-989-5555 belongs to $numbers{'1-888-989-5555'}\n";
```

Output of rev2.pl:

```
[student@OCS student]$ rev2.pl
The phone number 1-888-989-5555 belongs to ted:bob
```

Hashes of hashes

Suppose you want to keep track of data that is a bit more complex. For example, we want to keep track of a classroom of four students and the grades that each of them had throughout the year:

Student	Test #1	Homework #1	Homework #2
Joe	100	94	88
Sue	100	88	74
Nick	89	78	73
Fred	89	99	86

There are a few approaches that we can use to keep track of this information.

Approach #1 – Make four arrays, one for each student

```
@joe=(100, 94, 88);
@sue=(100, 88, 74);
@nick=(89, 78, 73);
@fred=(89, 99, 86);
```

While this does allow you to keep track of the student's grades, it is very cumbersome. For example, it is difficult to distinguish between a test and a homework grade. Also, how do you handle the data if a student misses a test or homework assignment? If all of the grades were the same and no assignments were ever skipped or missed, this might be a good solution. However, in most cases this is a very difficult way of handling the data.

Approach #2 – Make three associative arrays, one for each test

```
%test1=("Joe" => 100, "Sue" => 100, "Nick" => 89, "Fred" => 89);
%home1=("Joe" => 94, "Sue" => 88, "Nick" => 78, "Fred" => 99);
%home2=("Joe" => 88, "Sue" => 74, "Nick" => 73, "Fred" => 86);
```

Once again, while this will work, it is also pretty cumbersome technique to keep track of such data, especially if there are a lot of tests or homework assignments.

Approach #3 – Make a hash of hashes

The idea behind this approach is to make a hash that has references to hashes instead of regular scalars for the values. This approach will be covered in the next few sections.

Creating hashes of hashes

To create a hash of hashes that will store the data mentioned in the previous section, use the following syntax:

```
%scores = (
    Joe => {
```

```
        test1 => 100,
        homework1 => 94,
        homework2=> 88
    },
    Sue => {
        test1=> 100,
        homework1=> 88,
        homework2=> 74
    },
    Nick => {
        test1=> 89,
        homework1=> 78,
        homework2=> 73
    },
    Fred => {
        test1=> 89,
        homework1=> 99,
        homework2=> 86
    },
);
```

Note that you are really creating a hash with keys that contain referents to hash data. The referent is created when the value of the key is set to { }.

Accessing values in a hash of hashes

As with regular hashes, sometimes you want to access a single key's value and sometimes you want to transverse the entire hash, accessing all of the values of all of the keys. This section covered both of these methods.

Accessing one element

To access one element (to print, modify, add, etc.), use the following syntax:

$hash{key1}{key2}

For example, to access Joe's second grade (from the code in the previous section), use the following command:

```perl
print $scores{Joe}{homework2};
```

You can also use this syntax to modify Joe's second homework grade:

```perl
$scores{Joe}{ homework2}=76;
```

Or, you can add a new element using similar syntax:

```perl
$scores{Joe}{ homework3}=85;
```

The following example demonstrates these different techniques:

```perl
#!perl
#mkhash.pl

%scores = (
    Joe => {
        test1              => 100,
        homework1  => 94,
        homework2  => 88
    },
    Sue => {
        test1              => 100,
        homework1  => 88,
        homework2  => 74
    },
    Nick => {
        test1              => 89,
        homework1  => 78,
        homework2  => 73
    },
);
print "Joe's second homework grade: $scores{Joe}{ homework2}\n";

$scores{Joe}{ homework2}=97;

print "Joe's second homework grade: $scores{Joe}{ homework2}\n";
```

Output of mkhash.pl:

```
[student@OCS student]$ perl mkhash.pl
Joe's second homework grade: 88
Joe's second homework grade: 97
```

Accessing the entire hash

Use the following syntax to access the entire hash:

```perl
foreach $var1 (keys %hash) {
    print "$var1: ";
        foreach $var2 (keys %{$hash{$var1}}) {
            print "$var2 = $hash{$var1}{$var2} ";
        }
    print "\n";
}
```

For example, to print out the %scores grade in the preceding example, use the following code:

```perl
foreach $name (keys %scores) {
    print "$name: ";
        foreach $item (keys %{$scores{$name}}) {
            print "$item = $scores{$name}{$item} ";
        }
    print "\n";
}
```

Notes:

- ${$key1}{$key2} accesses an element in a hash of a hash (returns a scalar).
- %{$key1{$key2}} accesses the internal hash itself (returns a hash).

The following example demonstrates printing the entire hash:

```perl
#!perl
#hoh.pl
```

```
#create a hash of hash:
%scores = (
   Joe => {
      test1            => 100,
      homework1  => 94,
      homework2  => 88
   },
   Sue => {
      test1            => 100,
      homework1  => 88,
      homework2  => 74
   },
   Nick => {
      test1            => 89,
      homework1  => 78,
      homework2  => 73
   },
);

#print the hash of hash:

foreach $name (keys %scores) {
    print "$name: ";
        foreach $item (keys %{$scores{$name}}) {
           print "$item = $scores{$name}{$item} ";
        }
    print "\n";
}
```

Output of hoh.pl:

```
[student@OCS student]$ perl hoh.pl
Sue: homework2 = 74 test1 = 100 homework1 = 88
Nick: test1 = 89 homework1 = 78 homework2 = 73
Joe: homework2 = 88 test1 = 100 homework1 = 94
```

Other data structures

You are not limited to creating "arrays of arrays" or "hashes of hashes". You can also create "arrays of hashes", "hashes of arrays", "arrays of hashes of arrays", and so on.

Before determining the data structure that you will use, consider that the more complex the data structure, the more difficult it will be to maintain the code. With that in mind, you may want to limit the "depth" of your data structures.

The following example shows how to create and use a hash of arrays:

```perl
#!perl
#hoa.pl

#create a hash of arrays:
%scores = (
    Joe => [100, 94, 88],
    Sue => [100, 88, 74],
    Nick => [89, 78, 73],
    Fred => [89, 99, 86]
);
#print the hash of arrays:

foreach $name (keys %scores) {
    print "$name: ";
        foreach $item (@{$scores{$name}}) {
        print "$item ";
#or:
#        foreach $item (0..$#{$scores{$name}}) {
#        print "$scores{$name}[$item] ";
        }
    print "\n";
}
```

Output of hoa.pl:

```
[student@OCS student]$ perl hoa.pl
Fred: 89 99 86
Nick: 89 78 73
Joe: 100 94 88
Sue: 100 88 74
```

Revisiting reversing a hash

In a previous example in this unit, we saw how to reverse a hash manually. Given what we know now, it might be better to use a technique like the following which makes use of a hash of a hash structure:

```perl
#!perl
#rev3pl

%data=qw(bob 1-888-989-5555 ted 1-888-989-5555 sue 1-619-469-5555);

while (($key, $value) = each (%data)) {
   if (exists ($numbers{$value})) {
      push (@{$numbers{$value}}, $key);
   }
   else {
      $numbers{$value}=[$key];
   }
}

print "The phone number 1-888-989-5555 belongs to @{$numbers{'1-888-989--
5555'}}\n";
```

Output of rev3pl:

```
[student@OCS student]$ perl rev3.pl
The phone number 1-888-989-5555 belongs to ted bob
```

Additional resources

In each chapter, resources are provided to provide the learner with a source for more information. These resources may include downloadable source code or links to other books or articles that will provide you more information about the topic at hand.

Resources for this chapter can be found here:

```
https://github.com/apress/advanced-perl-programming
```

Lab exercises

Step #1

Create a script that uses hashes of hashes to keep track of salespeople's monthly sales amount. The hash's keys should be the salesperson's name (first and last), and the value should be another hash where the key is the month and year of the sales and the value is the amount of sales.

The script should allow the user the following options:

1. Add a new salesperson

2. Add a new record (salesperson's sales in a given month)

3. Print sales by salesperson

4. Print sales by month

5. Correct a record

6. Exit script

Step #2

If you finish the lab and still have time left, make the following improvements to your script:

1. Have the data saved into a file when the script ends.

2. Have the data read from your file into the hash when the script begins.

CHAPTER 5

Typeglobs

In order to understand globs, it's best to first understand what a symbolic table is. This will also help you understand packages and namespaces which are discussed in Chapter 7.

Perl uses symbolic tables to keep track of identifiers. An **identifier** is a name that is used by Perl to name items like variables, filehandles, and subroutines.

The symbolic table is basically a hash with a key for each identifier. Symbolic tables are stored in namespaces, which are also often called packages. By default, the symbolic table will store all of the identifiers for the program (except for "my" variables) in the "main" namespace. The use of the package command will provide Perl with multiple namespaces, each of which will have a separate symbolic table. Namespaces are covered in Chapter 7.

The use of symbolic tables is why Perl can have two (or more) different "data types" with the same name:

```
@names=qw(bob sue ted);
$names="Fred";
```

In the preceding example, the identifier "name" is used to identify two separate data types (an array and a scalar variable).

Virtual representation of a symbolic table

Suppose you executed the following code:

```
$names="Bob";
@names=qw(bob sue ted);
$age=25;
sub age {print "you are $age years old"};
```

© William "Bo" Rothwell of One Course Source, Inc. 2020
W. "Bo" Rothwell, *Advanced Perl Programming*, https://doi.org/10.1007/978-1-4842-5863-7_5

In a case such as this, we can represent the symbolic table like this:

Identifier	Data type	Value
names	Scalar	"Bob"
	Array	("bob", "sue", "ted")
	Hash	*Undef*
	Function	*Undef*
	Filehandle	*Undef*
age	Scalar	25
	Array	*Undef*
	Hash	*Undef*
	Function	{print "you are $age years old"};
	Filehandle	*Undef*

Typeglobs

The purpose of typeglobs is to provide a method to directly refer to an identifier within a symbolic table. Prior to the introduction of references to Perl, typeglobs were the most common method of "assigning by reference". The term for using typeglobs, however, is "alias", not "reference".

A later section will highlight the differences between references and typeglobs.

Using typeglobs
Making a typeglob

To make a typeglob, use the following syntax:

```
*typeglob=*identifier
```

Examples:

```
DB<1> @names=qw(bob sue ted)
DB<2> $names="Bob"
DB<3> *people=*names
```

Accessing the original variables via the alias

Once you have created a typeglob, you can access the original variables via the alias:

```
DB<1> @names=qw(bob sue ted)
DB<2> $names="Bob"
DB<3> *people=*names
DB<4> print $people
Bob
DB<5> print $people[2]
ted
```

Removing the alias

If you want to remove the typeglob, you can use the **undef** statement as follows:

```
DB<1> @names=qw(bob sue ted)
DB<2> $names="Bob"
DB<3> *people=*names
DB<4> print $people
Bob
DB<5> print $people[2]
ted
DB<6> undef *people
DB<7> print $people
DB<8> print $people[2]
```

Note You cannot use the statement "***people=undef**" to remove the typeglob. Although Perl won't return an error, this statement won't have any effect on the *people typeglob. The technique of assigning the return value of the **undef** statement using the assignment operator (the = sign) only works on scalar variables (or element of an array or values of a hash).

References vs. typeglobs

There are three primary differences between references and typeglobs:

1. A reference is made from a scalar variable to a single data type within another identifier, while typeglobs are made from one identifier to another identifier. In other words, if you make a reference to an associate array called %phone, no references are created to a scalar variable called $phone or any other data type within the "phone" identifier. With typeglobs, the alias is made to the entire identifier by default, not to a specific data type within the identifier.

   See the following for a visual example of this difference between references and typeglobs:

   ```
   $names="Bob";
   *people=*names;
   $person=\$names;
   ```

   In a case such as this, we can represent the symbolic table like this:

Identifier	Data type	Memory space address	Contents of memory space
names	Scalar	0x453f00	"Bob"
	Array	*N/A*	*N/A*
	Hash	*N/A*	*N/A*
	Function	*N/A*	*N/A*
	Filehandle	*N/A*	*N/A*
people	Scalar	"alias" to $names	NO MEMORY SPACE
	Array	"alias" to @names	NO MEMORY SPACE
	Hash	"alias" to %names	NO MEMORY SPACE
	Function	"alias" to &names	NO MEMORY SPACE
	Filehandle	"alias" to <names>	NO MEMORY SPACE

(continued)

Identifier	Data type	Memory space address	Contents of memory space
person	Scalar	0x342786	SCALAR 0x453f00
	Array	N/A	N/A
	Hash	N/A	N/A
	Function	N/A	N/A
	Filehandle	N/A	N/A

2. Another difference between references and typeglobs is that you can make references to "my" variables, but you can't make typeglobs to "my" variables. For example, consider the following program:

```perl
#!perl
#diff1.pl

###Using refs

{my($name)="Bob";
 $person=\$name;
 print "Example #1 \$name: $name\n";
 print "Example #1 \$\$person: $$person\n\n";
}

{my($age)=50;
 *years=*age;
 print "Example #2 \$age: $age\n";
 print "Example #2\$years: $years\n\n";
}
```

Note the output of the diff1.pl program. You can see how $$person acts as a reference to the "my" variable called $name, but $years is not a typeglob of $age:

```
[student@OCS student]$ diff1.pl
Example #1 $name: Bob
Example #1 $$person: Bob

Example #2 $age: 50
Example #2 $years:
```

71

3. The reason why references can be made to "my" variables is that references essentially share the same memory spaces as the "original" variables, while typeglobs are just aliases to another identifier.

    This is an important difference in cases like the following:

    ```perl
    #!perl
    #diff2.pl

    {my($name)="Bob";
    $person=\$name;
    my($age)=50;
    *years=*age;
    }
    print "\$name = $name\n";
    print "\$\$person = $$person\n";
    print "\$age = $age\n";
    print "\$years = $years\n";
    ```

    Output of diff2.pl:

    ```
    [student@OCS student]$ diff2.pl
    $name =
    $$person = Bob
    $age =
    $years =
    ```

    In the diff2.pl program, we were able to access the value of the "my" variable outside of the scope of the "my" variable. This is because the $$person reference "pointed to" the same memory space location as the "my" variable. Here is a visual representation of the diff2.pl program:

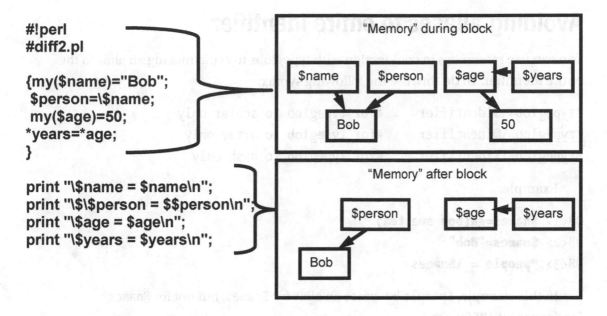

As you can see from the the diff2.pl program, there is a $years variable that is alias for the $age variable. However, since $age is not set in this scope, $years returns "undef". However, take a look at what happens if you assign $age variable:

```perl
#!perl
#diff3.pl

{my($name)="Bob";
 $person=\$name;
 my($age)=50;
*years=*age;
}

$age=100;
print "\$years = $years\n";
```

When you execute diff3.pl, you can see how the typeglob now displays the value from $age:

```
[student@OCS student]$ 5_diff3.pl
$years = 100
```

73

Avoiding aliases to entire identifier

You can use references in conjunction with typeglobs to avoid making an alias to the entire identifier. To do this, use the following syntax:

```
*typeglob=\$identifier      #for typeglob to scalar only
*typeglob=\@identifier      #for typeglob to array only
*typeglob=\%identifier      #for typeglob to hash only
```

Example:

```
DB<1> @names=qw(bob sue ted)
DB<2> $names="Bob"
DB<3> *people = \$names
```

In this example, $people becomes an alias for $names, but not for @names (or %names, <NAMES>, etc.).

Making constants

A useful aspect of typeglobs is that they provide you with a method of making constants. Perl doesn't provide a built-in constant type, but by using typeglobs and references, you can create a scalar variable that acts like a constant.

To make a constant, use the following technique:

```
*num=\10;
```

Once declared, you can access the value of the "constant" like you would a regular scalar variable:

```
DB<1> *num=\10
DB<2> print $num
10
```

If you attempt to modify the "constant", you will receive an error message:

```
DB<1> *num=\10
DB<2> print $num
10
DB<3> $num=5
```

*Modification of a read-only value attempted at (eval 6)[C:/Perl/lib/perl5db.pl:1
521] line 2.*

Passing filehandles into functions

Suppose you want to make a function that will read data from a filehandle. The filehandle
that the function will be opening will be passed into the function as an argument.
Unfortunately, Perl doesn't allow you to pass an actual filehandle as an argument.

Using typeglobs, you can assign a filehandle to a variable and pass this variable into a
function as an argument:

```perl
#!perl
#fh1.pl

sub read_data {
   $datafile=$_[0];
   $line=<$datafile>;
   print $line;
}

open (DATA, "<5_temp1.pl") || die;
$input=*DATA;
&read_data($input);
```

Be very careful as to how you work with this typeglob. In the previous example, the
subscript $_[0] was reassigned to the variable $datafile. This is because you can only
use a scalar variable with <>, not subscripts (or hashes, the outcome of statements, etc.).

You can also avoid the extra scalar assignment and directly pass in the typeglob:

```perl
#!perl
#fh2.pl

sub read_data {
   $datafile=$_[0];
   $line=<$datafile>;
   print $line;
}

open (DATA, "<5_temp1.pl") || die;
&read_data(*DATA);
```

Note   Modern versions of Perl allow you to store a filehandle directly in a variable:

```
open ($file, "<5_temp1.pl") || die;
```

If you use this technique, you are essentially doing the same thing as $file=*DATA.

Redefining a function

What happens when you attempt to run the following code?

```
#!perl
#redef1.pl
sub greet {
   print "hi there!\n";
}
&greet;
sub greet {
   print "welcome!\n";
}
&greet;
```

If you execute the preceding example, the result will look like this:

```
[student@OCS student]$ perl redef.pl
welcome!
welcome!
```

If you attempt to run the previous example with the **-w** switch, you will receive the following output:

```
[student@OCS student]$ perl redef1.pl
Subroutine greet redefined at 4_redef.pl line 10.
welcome!
welcome!
```

You often hear Perl programmers say "you can't redefine a function in Perl". It's a little more accurate to say "you can't redefine a function during runtime" using the **sub** statement. Functions are created during compile time, not runtime. The last function declaration in your script is the one that "sticks".

There are times when you may want to redefine a function during runtime. While Perl doesn't technically permit this, you can use typeglobs to simulate redeclaring a function during runtime:

```perl
#!perl
#redef2.pl

sub greet {
    print "hi there!\n";
}

&greet;

sub newgreet {
    print "welcome!\n";
}

*greet=\&newgreet;

&greet;
```

Output of redef2.pl:

```
[student@OCS student]$ perl redef2.pl
hi there!
welcome!
```

Redefining functions without using other functions

While you can redefine a function by using another existing function, this often isn't practical (and often not logical either). To redefine a function without using another function, use the syntax in the following example:

```perl
#!perl
#redef3.pl
```

```perl
sub greet {
    print "hi there!\n";
}

&greet;

*greet= sub {print "welcome!\n";};

&greet;
```

Temporarily redefining a function

While you can't use **my** on typeglobs, you can use **local**. Using the **local** statement in conjunction with blocks, you can temporarily redefine a function:

```perl
#!perl
#redef4.pl

sub greet {
    print "hi there!\n";
}

&greet;

{  #Begin block
local *greet= sub {print "welcome!\n";};

&greet;
}  #End block

&greet;
```

Nesting functions

Using a similar technique, you can nest functions. A nested function is one that is only callable within the subroutine that it is declared.

If you attempt to just define a function within a function, it won't result in a nested function; both functions will be callable throughout your program:

```perl
#!perl
#temp1.pl
sub print_total {
    sub show_values {
        print "5\n";
        print "7\n";
    }
    &show_values;
    print "The total is ", 5+7, "\n";
}

&print_total;
&show_values;
```

To make a true nested subroutine, use the following:

```perl
#!perl
#temp2.pl

sub print_total {
    local *show_values = sub {
        print "5\n";
        print "7\n";
    };
    &show_values;
    print "The total is ", 5+7, "\n";
}

&print_total;
&show_values;
```

Output of temp2.pl:

```
[student@OCS student]$ perl temp2.pl
5
7
The total is 12
Undefined subroutine &main::show_values called at temp2.pl line 14.
```

Additional resources

In each chapter, resources are provided to provide the learner with a source for more information. These resources may include downloadable source code or links to other books or articles that will provide you more information about the topic at hand.

Resources for this chapter can be found here:

https://github.com/apress/advanced-perl-programming

Lab exercises

Modify the script that you created in the Chapter 3 lab to include the following:

1. Instead of opening the filehandles within the subroutine, open them in the main program and pass them into the subroutine.

2. Using typeglob constants, limit the length of the "customer name" field to 25 characters.

## CHAPTER 6

Advanced Subroutine Handling

Subroutines are a fairly large topic in Perl. There are many features and nuances that allow you to create some powerful code. This chapter starts by reviewing some of the basic subroutine information that you should already know and then dives into more advanced subroutine features.

What you should already know about subroutines

Note   In the *Beginning Perl Programming* and *Pro Perl Programming* books, we covered some of the basics of subroutines. This section is meant to be a review of these topics.

The following function topics were covered in previous books:

1. Declaring subroutines

2. Invoking subroutines

3. Returning values from subroutines

4. Passing parameters info subroutines

5. Variable scope

6. my vs. local

7. use strict

8. Pre-declaring subroutines

© William "Bo" Rothwell of One Course Source, Inc. 2020
W. "Bo" Rothwell, *Advanced Perl Programming*, https://doi.org/10.1007/978-1-4842-5863-7_6

Declaring subroutines

To create a subroutine, use the **sub** statement:

```
sub total {
  print "The total is ", $a * $b + $c * $d, "\n";
}
```

Notes:

- Be careful when choosing subroutines' names. Perl has many built-in functions.

- Subroutines cannot be "redeclared" because they are created at compile time, not runtime (more on this later).

- By default, variables declared in your main program can be accessed and modified in your subroutines.

Invoking subroutines

To invoke (call) a subroutine, specify the ampersand character (&) followed by the subroutine's name:

```
sub total {
  print "The total is ", $a * $b + $c * $d, "\n";
}

$a=10;
$b=20;
$c=5;
$d=2;

&total;
```

The subroutine call doesn't really require the ampersand character. However, it is highly recommended that you place a "&" prior to subroutine calls because

1. It makes it easier for other programmers to see that this is a user-defined subroutine that is being called.

2. If you use the name of a Perl built-in subroutine and you **don't** use the "&" character, then the Perl built-in subroutine is called. If you **do** use the "&" character, then the subroutine you created will be called.

3. You can place your subroutines after the subroutine call if you call them with the "&" character (although this is not a good idea if you plan to implement scope with the **my** statement).

Returning values from functions

All subroutines return a value to the calling program. Although this return value is normally a scalar variable, it can also be an array or an associative array.

Two methods can be used to return a value to the calling program: the explicit method and the more cryptic implied method.

The explicit method

With the explicit method, use the **return** statement to specify what value to return to the calling program:

```
sub total {
  $total = $a * $b + $c * $d;
  return ($total);
}
```

You can either return the value of a variable or the outcome of a Perl statement:

```
sub total {
  return ($a * $b + $c * $d);
}
```

One of the advantages of using the **return** statement is that it is clear to another programmer what is being returned. Another advantage is that you can use the **return** statement to "pop out" of a subroutine prematurely:

```
sub test {
  if ($var =~ /ERROR/) {
    return (0);
  }
```

```
$result = $var;
chop ($result);
$result =~ s/^.../Pattern: /;
return ($result);
}
```

The implicit method

If you don't specify what to return with the **return** statement, Perl will return whatever the outcome of the last statement in the subroutine is:

```
sub total {
  $a * $b + $c * $d;
}
```

In this example, the outcome of the mathematical equation is returned. While this technique requires less typing, it doesn't provide any additional features and is a bit more cryptic than simply using the **return** statement.

Passing parameters

To pass parameters into a subroutine, place the parameters within parentheses after the subroutine call:

```
&average ($a, $b);
```

The variables $a and $b will be passed into the subroutine "average". Within the subroutine, you can access what was passed in by using the special array **@_**. The first parameter will be stored in $_[0], the second parameter will be stored in $_[1], and so on:

```
sub average {
    foreach $num (@_) {
        $total += $num;
    }
return ($total / ($#_+1));
}

$a=10;
$b=20;
print &average ($a, $b);        #prints 15
```

Notes:

- Just like any array, $#_ holds the last index number of @_.

- The parentheses around the arguments are not required.

Parameters are passed as references

When you pass a parameter into a subroutine, you actually pass a *reference*. The
elements in the **@_ array** are references to the variables that were passed into the
subroutine. Changing elements in the **@_ array** will also change the variables that are
being passed in:

```
sub average {
    $_[0]++;                          #Adds one to first element of _ array (and $a)
    foreach $num (@_) {
        $total += $num;
    }
return ($total / ($#_+1));
}

#main program
$a=10;
$b=20;
print &average ($a, $b);        #prints 15
print $a;                       #prints 11
```

To avoid this, you should reassign elements in @_ to other variables (either scalar or
another array):

```
sub average {
    @temp=@_;
    $temp[0]++;                              #Adds one to first element of temp array
    foreach $num (@temp) {
        $total += $num;
    }
return ($total / ($#temp+1));
}
```

```
#main program
$a=10;
$b=20;
print &average ($a, $b);          #prints 15
print $a;                         #prints 10
```

Scope of variables

By default, almost all variables in Perl are "global" in scope. This means that any
variable that you create in your main program can be accessed and modified by any
subroutine. While being able to have global variables is good for some situations, it can
cause problems when you (or fellow programmers) use the same variable name for
different reasons within the same script:

```
sub average {
   @temp=@_;
   $temp[0]++;                    #Adds one to first element of temp array
   foreach $num (@temp) {
      $total += $num;
   }
return ($total / ($#temp+1));
}

#main program
@temp=(10,20);
print &average ($a, $b);          #prints 15
print "@temp";                    #prints 11, 20
```

Perl does provide a couple of statements (**local** and **my**) that allow you to impose
scope on a variable. The idea of scope is to limit the "availability" of a variable to a
certain portion (typically a subroutine) of your script.

The local statement

The **local** statement can be used to protect the calling program's variables from being
modified from the subroutine:

```
sub average {
   local(@temp)=@_;                 #Main program's @temp isn't touched
   $temp[0]++;                      #Adds one to first element of local temp array
   foreach $num (@temp) {
      $total += $num;
   }
return ($total / ($#temp+1));
}

#main program
@temp=(10,20);
print &average ($a, $b);          #prints 15
print "@temp";                    #prints 10, 20
```

In the preceding example, the **local** statement makes a variable called @temp. This variable can't modify the @temp variable in the main program.

However, the **local** statement doesn't protect the subroutine's variables from being changed by other subroutines:

```
sub modify {
   @temp=(40,50);                #changes temp that was
                                 #created in average function

}
sub average {
   local(@temp)=@_;              #Main program's @temp isn't touched
   &modify;
   return (($temp[0] + $temp[1]) / 2);    #returns 45, result of 40 + 50 /2
}

#main program
@temp=(10,20);
print &average ($a, $b);         #prints 45
print "@temp";                   #prints 10, 20
```

A graphical representation:

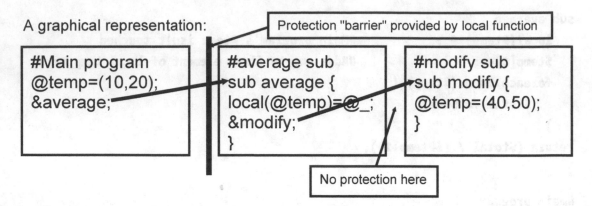

The my statement

The **my** statement is like the **local** statement in that it protects the calling program from having its variables modified by the subroutine. However, **my** also protects the subroutine from having its variable changed by another subroutine:

```
sub modify {
    @temp=(40,50);      #changes temp, but not the average sub's temp
}

sub average {
    my(@temp)=@_;        #Main program's @temp isn't touched
    &modify;
    return (($temp[0] + $temp[1]) / 2);      #returns 15
}

#main program
@temp=(10,20);
print &average ($a, $b);        #prints 15
print "@temp";                  #prints 40, 50
```

#Main program @temp=(10,20); &average;	#average sub sub average { my(@temp)=@_; &modify; }	Protection "barrier"
		#modify sub sub modify { @temp=(40,50); }

The bad "side effect" of the preceding example is that when the modify subroutine assigns the @temp variable, it ends up modifying the main program ("global") @temp variable. To avoid this, either use the **my** statement when creating the main program's variables or use the **my** statement when creating the modify subroutine's variables (or even better, do both!):

```
sub modify {
   my(@temp)=(40,50);    #changes modify's temp
}

sub average {
   my(@temp)=@_;            #Main program's @temp isn't touched
   &modify;
   return (($temp[0] + $temp[1]) / 2);    #returns 15
}

#main program
my(@temp)=(10,20);
print &average ($a, $b);     #prints 15
print "@temp";               #prints 10, 40
```

use strict

There are three things you can tell Perl to be strict about: reference usage, subroutine usage, and variable usage. This is a review of the **"use strict 'subs'"** statement.

The "use strict 'subs'" statement creates an error message for barewords (strings without quotes around them) that don't call a valid subroutine. Example:

```
#!perl
#subs.pl

use strict 'subs';

sub jesttest {
  print "This is just a test";
}

sub hello {
print "hello\n";
}
```

```
hello;          #Calls a valid subroutine, no problem
justatest;      #Bareword that isn't a subroutine.
```

Note the compile-time errors in the output of subs.pl:

[student@OCS student]$ **perl subs.pl**

Bareword "justatest" not allowed while "strict subs" in use at subs.pl
line 15.
Execution of subs.pl aborted due to compilation errors.

Pre-declaring subroutines

Typically, you need to declare a subroutine prior to using it. For example, the following
code won't produce any output since the subroutine isn't declared until after it is called:

```
#!perl
#sub1.pl

hello;

sub hello {
    print "hi there\n";
}
```

This can cause problems, especially if you are using "use strict":

```
#!perl
#sub2.pl

use strict subs;

hello;

sub hello {
    print "hi there\n";
}
```

Because the previous program uses the 'use strict subs' pragma, the program
fails with a compile-time error message:

[student@OCS student]$ **perl sub2.pl**

Bareword "hello" not allowed while "strict subs" in use at sub2.pl line 6.
Execution of sub2.pl aborted due to compilation errors.

Using **"use subs"**, you can "predefine" subroutines:

```
#!perl
#sub3.pl
use subs qw(hello);
use strict subs;

hello;

sub hello {
   print "hi there\n";
}
```

Notice that the program now works, and you are able to put your subroutine at the bottom of the program:

```
[student@OCS student]$ perl sub3.pl
```

hi there

If you are wondering "why didn't we just put the subroutine at the top of the program and avoid this problem altogether?", then consider this: when reading a program that either you or someone else writes, the first place you should start is the beginning of the main part of the program. Having a bunch of functions at the top of the program means you have to scan past all of the functions, hunting for the main part of the program. In other words, having the functions at the bottom part of the program makes the program more readable.

There is, however, a cost associated with this technique and it comes when using my variables. This cost (and the solution) will be covered later in this book.

Notes:

- Once invoked, you cannot use **"no subs"** to undo a **"use subs"** statement.

- If you use the ampersand character before the function name, you do not have to predeclare subroutines that are placed after they are called. More on this in a later discussion on the difference between using the & character when calling a function and not using the & character.

What you might know about subroutines

Based on your experiences with Perl, you may have picked up the following.

Functions vs. subroutines

Basically, there isn't a distinction in Perl between the terms "function" and "subroutine". In fact, the terms are often used interchangeably in Perl.

In some languages, a subroutine doesn't return a value while a function does. In other languages, a subroutine doesn't explicitly return a value while a function does.

In Perl, all functions return a value (even if it is "undef") even if most programmers use the implicit method to return this value.

Note   You might also hear the term method. A method is an object-oriented version of a subroutine. In other words, a method is a subroutine that knows what class it belongs to.

Parameters are passed in as a single flat list

When you pass parameters into a function, they are all passed in as a single flat list. Even if these parameters are arrays or hashes, they are passed into the function as a single flat list.

Using references, you can pass parameters into a function as arrays or hashes. This will be covered in a future section in this chapter.

Return values are passed out in a single flat list

Return values are also passed out as a single flat list. We will cover how you can return values as individual arrays or hashes in a later section.

Reassigning the @_ `array` breaks the references

As mentioned before, parameters are passed into the function as references. Changing the @_ array within the function modifies the value of the parameters that were passed into the function.

However, if you assign the entire @_ array, the @_ array link to the references is broken and no changes are made to the parameters that were passed into the function:

```perl
#!perl
#break1.pl

sub test {
    print "In the function: ", "@_", "\n";
    @_=qw(abc xyz);   #breaks the "link"
    print "In the function: ","@_", "\n";
}

@colors=qw(red blue yellow);
&test(@colors);
print "Out of the array: ", "@colors", "\n";
```

Output of break1.pl:

```
[student@OCS student]$ break1.pl
In the function: red blue yellow
In the function: abc xyz
Out of the array: red blue yellow
```

To break the link to the calling scope's variables, but get a copy of the data, use the following method:

```perl
#!perl
#break.pl

sub test {
    print "In the function: ", "@_", "\n";
    $_[0]="purple";
    print "In the function: ","@_", "\n";
    @_=@_;   #breaks the "link"
    $_[1]="orange";
    print "In the function: ","@_", "\n";
}

@colors=qw(red blue yellow);
&test(@colors);
print "Out of the array: ", "@colors", "\n";
```

The @_ `array` can be inherited from the calling program

If you call up a function by using the "&" character and you don't pass any parameters
into the function, then the @_array of the calling program is automatically passed in:

```perl
#!perl
#in.pl

sub test {
    print "In the test function: ", "@_", "\n";
}

sub pass {
    print "In the pass function: ", "@_", "\n";
    &test;
}

@colors=qw(red blue yellow);
&pass (@colors);
```

Output of in.pl (note that the test function has the same parameters that were
passed into the pass function):

```
[student@OCS student]$ in.pl
In the pass function: red blue yellow
In the test function: red blue yellow
```

Note   If you don't use the "&" character when calling the function, then @_ of the
calling program isn't passed into the function.

---

my variables affect blocks, not just subroutines

Most Perl programmers learn about the **my** statement when trying to "protect" their
function's variables. While the **my** statement is definitely useful for this, it also is useful in
other cases.

The **my** statement makes a variable visible only to the block it is created in:

```perl
#!perl
#my1.pl
$name="Bob";

{
my $name = "Tim";   #var only exists within block
print "$name\n";
}
print "$name\n";
```

Output of my1.pl (note that the value of the $name variable changes based on scope):

```
[student@OCS student]$ my1.pl
Tim
Bob
```

This can be somewhat confusing when dealing with conditional statements:

```perl
#!perl
#my2.pl
while (my $line = <STDIN>) {
    print "$. $line";
}
```

In this case, the scope of the **my** variable is the scope of the **while** loop itself.

You can't my all variables

Not all variables can be made into **my** variables. Only alphanumeric (typically thought of as user-defined) variables can be "myed". Special variables (such as $_ and $|) cannot be "myed".

This doesn't mean that you can't have scope on special variables. As we will see in a future section, you can use the **local** statement to impose scope on special variables.

my variables are not created until after the statement is complete

This is a small issue, but an important one. Suppose you executed the following script:

```perl
#!perl
#my3.pl

$name="Bob";

{
    my  $name=$name;
    print "$name\n";
    $name="Ted";
    print "$name\n";
}

print "$name\n";
```

The value of $name *while* the line "my $name=$name" is being executed is "Bob". It is only *after* the line is finished being executed that $name becomes a **my** variable.

This is a useful bit of knowledge as you can use it to initialize a my variable with the "old" value of the variable. Otherwise, the new my variable would be undefined initially.

Nested functions have their own my variables

This is another small but important point. If you have a function that calls itself and within this function there is a **my** variable declared, each function call contains a separate value for this variable. Executing the following code will show how this works:

```perl
#!perl
#nest.pl

sub setvar {
    my $value = $i;
    print "$value\n";
    $i=10;
    &setvar if ($value == 20);
    print "$value\n";
}
```

```
$i=20;
&setvar;
```

Output of nest.pl (note how each subroutine call has a separate value for the **my** variable):

```
[student@OCS student]$ nest.pl
20
10
10
20
```

Foreach loops use local variable, but they can be my variables

By default, when you create a **foreach** loop, the assignment variable is created as a local variable:

```
foreach $var (@colors) {print "$var\n";}
```

In the preceding example, $var is local to the **foreach** statement. In most cases, this is fine. In fact, it can even be useful:

```
#!perl
#foreach1.pl

$var="CODE BLACK";

sub printit {
    print "$var\n";
}

@colors=qw(red blue green);

foreach $var (@colors) {
    &printit;
}

print "$var\n";
```

Why is it useful that the $var in the **foreach** loop is a local variable by default? Because if it wasn't, then the original $var variable would be changed in the foreach loop and the result of the last **print** statement would be "green", not "CODE BLACK" as shown in the following output:

```
[student@OCS student]$ perl foreach1.pl
red
blue
green
CODE BLACK
```

However, the fact that the variable is a local variable by default can also cause problems. Consider the following code:

```
#!perl
#foreach2.pl

sub changeit {
    $var="brown";
}

@colors=qw(red blue green);

foreach $var (@colors) {
    &changeit;
}

print "@colors","\n";
```

So, why is this a problem? Because the $var variable in the **foreach** loop is a local variable, that means any subroutine call done within the **foreach** loop is able to modify this variable. And because the $var variable is a reference to values in the @colors array, changes to the $var variable end up changing the original array as shown in the following output:

```
[student@OCS student]$ foreach2.pl
brown brown brown
```

You can have your assignment variable in a foreach loop be a **my** variable instead:

```perl
#!perl
#foreach3.pl

$var="CODE BLACK";

sub changeit {
    $var="brown";
}

@colors=qw(red blue green);

foreach my $var (@colors) {
    &changeit;
}

print "@colors","\n";
print "$var\n";
```

The output of foreach3.pl demonstrates protection of both the original $var variable and the $var variable within the **foreach** loop (and, as a result, protection of the @colors array):

```
[student@OCS student]$ foreach3.pl
red blue green
CODE BLACK
```

Notes:

- This technique can also be applied to **for** loops.

- If you are using the 'my strict vars' pragma, then you must use **my** variables in **foreach** loops as this pragma does not permit **local** variables.

While **my** is preferred, `local` is still useful

In most cases, you want to create **my** variables, not **local** variables. There are a few notable exceptions:

1. You can't make special variables **my** variables, but you can make them **local** variables. This can be useful when you want to modify special variables temporarily.

    For example, suppose you want to temporarily change the default variable ($_) variable. You can execute the following code:

    ```perl
    #!perl
    #local1.pl

    $_=<STDIN>;

    print "Before the block:\n";
    print $_;
    {local ($_);
     $_=<STDIN>;
     print "In the block:\n";
     print $_;}

    print "After the block:\n";
    print $_;
    ```

2. You can use the **local** statement to create localized filehandle or function. Remember the following example from Chapter 5:

    ```perl
    #!perl
    #redef4.pl

    sub greet {
        print "hi there!\n";
    }

    &greet;

    {   #Begin block
    local *greet= sub {print "welcome!\n";};
    ```

```perl
&greet;
}   #End block

&greet;
```

3. You can use the **local** statement to temporarily change part of an array or hash. For example:

```perl
#!perl

#local2.pl

@colors=qw(red blue yellow);

{local $colors[1]="Purple";

 print "$colors[1]\n";

 print "@colors", "\n";

}

print "$colors[1]\n";

print "@colors", "\n";
```

Note   Making $colors[0] a local variable doesn't have any impact on the rest of the elements in the array:

```perl
@colors=qw(red blue yellow);
{local $colors[0]="purple";
print "$colors[0]\n;    #prints "purple"
print $colors[1]\n";    #prints "blue"
}
print "$colors[0]\n;    #prints "red";
```

You might now be thinking "But, shouldn't we always use the 'use strict vars' pragma?" The answer to that is "yes, except in those places in your code when a local variable actually makes sense". So, you should start your program by using the 'use strict vars' pragma, then turn off this pragma when you need to use a local variable, then turn it back on again. For example:

```perl
#!perl
#local3.pl

use strict vars;

$_=<STDIN>;

print "Before the block:\n";
print $_;

no strict vars;
{local ($_);
 $_=<STDIN>;
 print "In the block:\n";
 print $_;}
use strict vars;

print "After the block:\n";
print $_;
```

Note   The author normally uses the `'use strict vars'` pragma by default
(actually, he uses the `'use strict'` pragma for all three "`strict`" features).
In this book, this statement was omitted in all code by default unless there was a
purpose to discussing this pragma.

Making persistent function variables

In some languages, there is a built-in method for having a function's variable retain
its value between calls. However, Perl's default behavior is to **undef** private variables
(variables created with my) each time the function is called as demonstrated by the
following code:

```perl
#!perl
#persistent1.pl

sub keep_data {
```

```perl
    if (defined ($var)) {
       print "\$var is defined\n";
    }
    my $var=10;
}

&keep_data;
&keep_data;
```

There would be no output of the previous code since the $var variable is never defined when the keep_data function is called.

Remember that what the **my** statement does is to maintain the value of the variable within the scope that it was declared in. In the case of a function call, the scope is the function itself.

If, however, you create a block around the function, you can declare a variable that is private to the function and maintains its value from one function call to another:

```perl
#!perl
#persistent2.pl

{
    my $var;
    sub keep_data {

      if (defined ($var)) {
         print "\$var is defined\n";
      }
      $var=10;
    }
}

print "Result of first call: \n";
&keep_data;
print "Result of second call: \n";
&keep_data;
print "value of \$var: $var\n";
```

Note that in the first call $var hasn't been defined yet (it is a **my** variable, but not defined), but in the second call $var is defined. Therefore, the variable is persistent. Additionally, it is not available anywhere except in the subroutine as you can see when the final print statement in the main program is executed:

```
[student@OCS student]$ perl persistent2.pl
Result of first call:
Result of second call:
$var is defined
value of $var:
```

You might be wondering "how did the **my** variable survive between function calls?" Once the **my** variable has been created, it stays in existence until all code within the scope of the **my** variable has been executed. Because you can call the function during the entire program, there is always executable code "housed" with the scope of the **my** variable, so the variable is not destroyed until the end of the program. But, it is only accessible within the scope that it was created, which means only that function can access that variable. The result: a persistent and private variable.

Hopefully, you are thinking to yourself "but, wait a minute, Perl does now offer a technique to create persistent private variables". And you would be right because as of Perl 5.10 you can use the 'use feature "state"' pragma to allow you to create persistent variables with the **state** statement. This and other new features will be covered in Chapter 13.

The 'use feature "state"' pragma provides an excellent quick way to create persistent variables. However, consider the following code:

```perl
#!perl
#persistent3.pl

{
    my $var;
    sub test1 {
        $var=10;
    }
    sub test2 {
        print "In test2: $var\n";
    }
}
```

```perl
sub test3 {
    print "In test3: $var\n";
}

&test1;
&test2;
&test3;
```

Now in persistent3.pl, we have a persistent "shared" private variable! Because $var was created in the same scope as that of the test1 and test2 functions, they can both access this private variable, and it is persistent. This is a feature that the 'use feature "state"' pragma does not provide.

Using the caller function

The **caller** function provides information such as package name (see future Unit on packages), filename, function name, and other data.

The caller function returns an array of ten elements. While some of these elements are very useful, others are not all that important. The following chart illustrates the ten elements that are returned:

Element	Value
0	Contains the package name that the code was compiled in. See more on packages in Chapter 7
1	Contains the filename that the code was compiled in. If the script was executed with the **-e** option, the value of this element is set to **-e**
2	Contains the line number that the function was called from
3	Contains the complete function name (including package)
4	Contains 0 if the function was called without arguments; contains 1 if the function was called with arguments
5	Contains the value of **wantarray**. See more on **wantarray** in a future section
6	Is unset if the code is not being called by the **eval** statement; contains data if the code is being called by the **eval** statement
7	Is set to true if code is called by **require** or **use** statements
8	Not intended for external use
9	Not intended for external use

When you use the **caller** statement, you need to pass it a numeric value to specify exactly what values to return. This number is useful when you have nested loops. The value of 0 provides data about your function. The value of 1 provides data about the function that called your function.

In the following example, the data about the display_data function is printed:

```perl
#!perl
#caller.pl

sub display_data {
   @info=caller(0);
   foreach $data (@info) {
      print $i++, "\t$data\n";
   }

}

&display_data;
```

Output of caller.pl:

```
[student@OCS student]$ perl caller.pl
0    main
1    caller.pl
2    12
3    main::display_data
4    0
5
```

Passing arguments by reference

To begin with, we already pointed out that arguments are already passed into functions by reference. However, the method that Perl uses might not be the way you want them passed.

For example, consider the following code:

```perl
#!perl
#ref1.pl
```

```perl
sub print_array {
    for ($i=0; $i <= $#_ ; $i++) {
        print "$i\t$_[$i]\n";
    }
}

@colors=qw(red blue yellow green);
@col=qw(pink purple black);

&print_array(@colors, @col);
```

Note the output of ref1.pl:

```
[student@OCS student]$ perl ref1.pl
0       red
1       blue
2       yellow
3       green
4       pink
5       purple
6       black
```

While the arrays @colors and @col are passed in as references, they aren't passed in as separate references. Each element in the @_ array is a reference to an element in either @colors or @col. In other words, there isn't any way to distinguish between the two arrays within the function.

If you need to be able to distinguish between arrays (or hashes) that are passed into a function, pass them in as references yourself. Example:

```perl
#!perl
#ref2.pl

sub print_array {
    ($first, $second)=@_;
    print "First array:\n";
    for ($i=0; $i < @$first ; $i++) {
        print "$i\t$$first[$i]\n";
    }
    print "Second array:\n";
```

```
    for ($i=0; $i < @$second ; $i++) {
        print "$i\t$$second[$i]\n";
    }

}

@colors=qw(red blue yellow green);
@col=qw(pink purple black);

&print_array(\@colors, \@col);
```

As you can see from the output of ref2.pl, you are now able to treat the arguments as two separate array references:

```
[student@OCS student]$ ref2.pl
First array:
0       red
1       blue
2       yellow
3       green
Second array:
0       pink
1       purple
2       black
```

Determining functions return data

Consider the following two statements:

```
$var=&sub;
@var=&sub;
```

In the first statement, you are assigning a scalar variable to the return value of &sub. In the second statement, you are assigning an array variable to the return value of &sub.

There is an important difference between the two statements. To better understand this difference, first consider the following program:

```
#!perl
#want1.pl
```

```perl
sub return_data {
    @colors=qw(red blue yellow green);
    return (@colors);
}

$result=&return_data;
print "$result\n";

@result=&return_data;
print "@result","\n";
```

When this program is executed, the following results are printed:

```
[student@OCS student]$ perl want1.pl
4
red blue yellow green
```

The line "$result=&return_data" assigned the value "4" to $result because when array data is returned in scalar context, the value returned is the number of elements in the array, not the data in the array.

Many Perl statements return different values if they are called in scalar context than if they are called in array context. To take advantage of this with your own functions, use the **wantarray** statement.

The **wantarray** statement can return one of three values:

- true if function is called in array context

- false if function is called in scalar context

- undef if function return value isn't requested

Syntax of **wantarray**:

```perl
if (wantarray) {                    #if true, need to return an array
    return (@array);
}
elsif (defined (wantarray)) {       #if true, need to return a scalar
    return ($scalar);
}
else {                              #don't need to return anything
    return;
}
```

Take a look at the following example of **wantarray**:

```perl
#!perl
#want2.pl

sub return_data {
    @colors=qw(red blue yellow green);
    if (wantarray) {
        return (@colors);
    }
    elsif (defined (wantarray)) {
        return ($colors[0]);
    }
    else {
    return;
    }
}

$result=&return_data;
print "$result\n";

@result=&return_data;
print "@result","\n"; of elements in the array, not the data in the array.
array data is returned in scalar context, the val
```

Notice how the output of the return_data function in the want2.pl is different depending on how it is called:

```
[student@OCS student]$ perl want2.pl
red
red blue yellow green
```

Returning multiple values

Just as arguments to a function are passed in as a single array, return values are passed out as a single array. If you need to return a set of arrays (or hashes), use references:

```perl
sub whatever {
    #code here
    return (\@array1, \@array2);
}
```

In the calling program, you want to assign the return values to scalar variables

```perl
($var1, $var2) = &function;
```

or another array

```perl
@array=&function;
```

What you don't want to do is the following:

```perl
(@array1, @array2)=&function;
```

This will put both references in the @array1 array and nothing in @array2.
Example of using this feature:

```perl
#!perl
#ret1.pl

sub return_data {
    @colors1=qw(red blue yellow green);
    @colors2=qw(purple teal aqua orange);
    return (\@colors1, \@colors2);
}

($first, $second)=&return_data;

print "First element of first array: $$first[0]\n";
print "First element of second array: $$second[0]\n";
```

Output of ret1.pl:

```
[student@OCS student]$ ret1.pl
red
purple
```

> **Note**   This is a drawback to using this technique. If you are writing the
> function that returns the array references, then whoever uses your code needs
> to understand how to deal with references or you need to provide a little
> documentation on how to call your function. For example, you could provide the
> following example.

```
#First, call my function
($first, $second)=&return_data;

#Next, assign the variables to regular arrays:
@first=@$first;
@second=@$second;

#Lastly, undef the original variables since you don't need them any more:
undef $first;
undef $second;
```

Exception handling

Suppose you have the following program:

```
#!perl
#ex1.pl

sub result {
    print "Please enter the first number: ";
    $num1=<STDIN>;
    print "Please enter the second number: ";
    $num2=<STDIN>;
    return ($num1 / $num2);
}

print "The result is ", &result, "\n";
```

Notice the sample output of ex1.pl when "good" values are provided by the user:

```
[student@OCS student]$ ex1.pl
Please enter the first number: 4
Please enter the second number: 5
The result is 0.8
```

The program runs just great... until the user who is running the program types "0" for the second number:

```
[student@OCS student]$ ex1.pl
Please enter the first number: 4
Please enter the second number: 0
Illegal division by zero at ex1.pl line 9, <STDIN> line 2.
```

Division by zero is a runtime error. Obviously, an easy way to prevent this error is to check the value of the second number prior to executing the **return** statement. Some runtime errors, however, are not so easy to "pick up".

Another method would be to call the function using the **eval** statement. Any runtime errors that occur within a **eval** call do not cause your script to exit prematurely. They do, however, assign the error message to the $@ variable which you can use to determine what action to take.

In this example, we call the function using **eval** to avoid premature aborting of our script:

```
#!perl
#ex2.pl

sub result {
    print "Please enter the first number: ";
    $num1=<STDIN>;
    print "Please enter the second number: ";
    $num2=<STDIN>;
    return ($num1 / $num2);
}

eval {$output = &result};
```

```perl
if ($@) {
    print "An error occurred: $@";
}
else {
    print "The result is ", $output, "\n";
}
```

Example outputs of running ex2.pl with both "good" input and "bad" input:

*[student@OCS student]$ **ex2.pl***
Please enter the first number: 4
Please enter the second number: 0
An error occurred: Illegal division by zero at ex2.pl line 9, <STDIN> line 2.
*[student@OCS student]$ **ex2.pl***
Please enter the first number: 4
Please enter the second number: 5
The result is 0.8

You might think to yourself "this doesn't seem much different", but that is just because in ex2.pl the value of $@ was printed. What is different is that if there was more code in the program, it would continue to execute. Also, you don't have to print the value of $@; you could take any action you want if the code in the **eval** statement fails.

Constant functions

In Chapter 5, we used typeglobs and references to make a constant. While that is a popular method of making a constant, using functions to create a constant is also a popular method.

The following example will create a constant function, but it isn't the most efficient method:

```perl
#!perl
#const1.pl

sub pi {3.14159}

print "The value of pi is about ", pi, "\n";
```

Output of const1.pl:

```
[student@OCS student]$ const1.pl
The value of pi is about 3.14159
```

A more efficient method is to use an "in line" function. In line functions are very quick since they don't accept any arguments:

```perl
#!perl
#const2.pl

sub pi () {3.14159}

print "The value of pi is about ", pi, "\n";
```

The output of const2.pl is no different than const2.pl, but by using prototypes, the function is more efficient (more on prototypes later in this chapter):

```
[student@OCS student]$ const2.pl
The value of pi is about 3.14159
```

There is one more method of making a constant. The built-in Perl module "constant.pm" can be used to create a constant:

```perl
#!perl
#const3.pl

use constant PI => 3.14159;

print "The value of pi is about ", PI, "\n";
```

Output of const3.pl:

```
[student@OCS student]$ const3.pl
The value of pi is about 3.14159
```

Notes:

- The **use constant** statement makes an in line function just like we did in the previous examples.

- The biggest difference between constant functions and constant typeglobs is that constant functions are declared at compile time, while constant typeglobs are declared during runtime.

Prototypes

The purpose of prototypes is to set parameters on the arguments that are being passed into your function. For example, suppose your function needed exactly two scalar arguments:

```perl
#!perl
#proto1.pl

sub switch ($$) {
    return ($_[1], $_[0]);
}

$a=10;
$b=20;
($a, $b) = switch ($a, $b);
print "\$a = $a\n";
print "\$b = $b\n";
```

Each $ represents a single scalar that should be passed into the function. As you can see in the output of proto1.pl, there are no problems:

```
[student@OCS student]$ proto1.pl
$a = 20
$b = 10
```

The ($$) in the function declaration told Perl that there should only be two scalar arguments passed into the function. If more than two scalar arguments are passed, a runtime error occurs:

```perl
#!perl
#proto2.pl

sub switch ($$) {
    return ($_[1], $_[0]);
}

$a=10;
$b=20;
$c=30;
```

```perl
($a, $b) = switch ($a, $b, $c);

print "\$a = $a\n";
print "\$b = $b\n";
```

The output of proto2.pl demonstrates the runtime error:

[student@OCS student]$ **proto2.pl**
Too many arguments for main::switch at proto2.pl line 12, near "$c)"
Execution of proto2.pl aborted due to compilation errors.

Also, if not enough arguments are passed, a runtime error occurs:

```perl
#!perl
#proto3.pl

sub switch ($$) {
    return ($_[1], $_[0]);
}

$a=10;

($a, $b) = switch ($a);

print "\$a = $a\n";
print "\$b = $b\n";
```

Output of proto3.pl:

[student@OCS student]$ **proto3.pl**
Not enough arguments for main::switch at proto3.pl line 10, near "$a)"
Execution of proto3.pl aborted due to compilation errors.

As it stands, the prototype method we are using isn't foolproof. Consider the following example:

```perl
#!perl
#proto4.pl

sub switch ($$) {
    return ($_[1], $_[0]);
}
```

117

```perl
@nums=(10, 20, 30, 40, 50);
$c=30;

($a, $b) = switch (@nums, $c);

print "\$a = $a\n";
print "\$b = $b\n";
```

Now take a look at the output of proto4.pl:

```
[student@OCS student]$ proto4.pl
$a = 30
$b = 5
```

In this example, the @nums parameter is "treated as" a scalar value because your prototype told Perl that it needed to pass in two scalar values. When an array is treated as a scalar (a.k.a. scalar context), the number of elements in the array is the return value. As a result, the first argument passed into the switch function is 5, not the values of the array.

To avoid this potential problem, you can tell Perl that the original value must itself be a scalar (not referenced as a scalar) by putting a "\" in front of the prototype:

```perl
#!perl
#proto5.pl

sub switch (\$\$) {
    return ($_[1], $_[0]);
}

@nums=(10, 20, 30, 40, 50);
$c=30;

($a, $b) = switch (@nums, $c);

print "\$a = $a\n";
print "\$b = $b\n";
```

The output of proto5.pl now results in an error:

```
[student@OCS student]$ proto5.pl
Type of arg 1 to main::switch must be scalar (not array deref) at proto5.pl
line 11, near "$c)"
Execution of proto5.pl aborted due to compilation errors.
```

Prototype characters

The following chart illustrates the prototype characters:

Character	Meaning
$	Expects a scalar
\$	Requires a scalar
;$	An optional scalar
@	Expects an array
\@	Requires an array
;@	An optional array
%	Expects a hash
&	Expects a subroutine
*	Expects a typeglob

Notes:

- The "\" and ";" characters can be used with all types, not just scalars and arrays.

- If you specify "()", you are telling Perl to not accept any arguments.

119

Additional resources

In each chapter, resources are provided to provide the learner with a source for more information. These resources may include downloadable source code or links to other books or articles that will provide you more information about the topic at hand.

Resources for this chapter can be found here:

```
https://github.com/apress/advanced-perl-programming
```

Lab exercises

Take the script that you created in the Chapter 5 lab and make the following changes:

1. Implement `"use strict'subs'"`.

2. If you have any `"global"` variables, make them into `"my"` variables (with the exception of the array that contains the open ticket data, the typeglob constant, and the `$clear` variable, if you have one).

3. Change all of your `foreach` loops to use `my` variables instead of `local` variables.

CHAPTER 7

Packages and Namespaces

Novice Perl programmers typically are told that Perl has no scope by default. While not technically accurate, without packages, variables in Perl appear to be global.

Technically, most variables are not "global". Variables are stored in "namespaces" which are created by packages.

One package exists by default: the main package. To prevent accidentally overwriting variables that exist in other portions of the script, you can create additional namespaces with the **package** command.

If you create a Perl module that will be called by another Perl program, you should always place your variables in a different package than the main package.

Creating namespaces with the **package** command

To tell Perl to switch to a different package, use the **package** command as demonstrated in the following program:

```perl
#!perl
#pack1.pl

$name="Bob";
print "name = $name\n";

package New;
print "name = $name\n";

$name="Ted";
print "name = $name\n";

package main;
print "name = $name\n";
```

© William "Bo" Rothwell of One Course Source, Inc. 2020
W. "Bo" Rothwell, *Advanced Perl Programming*, https://doi.org/10.1007/978-1-4842-5863-7_7

```
package New;
print "name = $name\n";
```

While reviewing pack1.pl, notice the output of the program:

```
[student@OCS student]$ perl pack1.pl
name = Bob
name =
name = Ted
name = Bob
name = Ted
```

Notes:

- Package names start with a capital letter by convention. While this isn't a requirement, it is generally considered good style. The main package, however, is in all lowercase letters.

- In addition to variables, other identifiers are stored in namespaces: functions, typeglobs, and so on.

Fully qualified package names

Even if you change to a different package, you can still access identifiers from the main package (or any other package). To do this, you will have to use fully qualified package names.

You can think of a fully qualified package name much like a full pathname in a UNIX or DOS shell. In a UNIX shell, you use a slash key to separate the name of the files and the directories (or backslash in DOS). In Perl, you use the ":: " symbol to separate the name of the package and the identifier:

```
#!perl
#pack2.pl

$name="Bob";
print "name = $name\n";

package New;
print "main::name = $main::name\n";
$name="Ted";
print "name = $name\n";
```

Output of pack2.pl:

```
[student@OCS student]$ perl pack2.pl
name = Bob
main::name = Bob
name = Ted
```

Note   The identifier $main::var can also be written as $::var.

Alternative method

The "old" method of specifying fully qualified variable name was to use a single quote instead of double colons. This means that the preceding example can be rewritten like this:

```
#!perl
#pack3.pl

$name="Bob";
print "name = $name\n";

package New;
print "main'name = $main'name\n";
$name="Ted";
print "name = $name\n";
```

Because of this, the following statement will produce an "unusual" result:

```
print "This is $person's new car\n";
```

This will print the $s variable from the "person" package.

Nested packages

You can (kind of) have a package nested within another package, what you might consider to be a "nested" package. Note: The following is *not* an example of declaring a package within another package. In this example, we just switch from one package to another:

123

```perl
#!perl
#nest1.pl

$name="Bob";
print "name = $name\n";

package New;
$name="Ted";

package Data;
$name="Fred";

package main;
print "name=$New::name\n";
print "name=$Data::name\n";
```

Output of nest1.pl:

```
[student@OCS student]$ nest1.pl
name = Bob
name=Ted
name=Fred
```

Declaring "nested" packages

To declare a package "within" another package, use the following syntax:

```perl
#!perl
#nest2.pl

$name="Bob";
print "name = $name\n";

package New;
$name="Ted";

package New::Data;
$name="Fred";

package main;
print "name=$New::name\n";
print "name=$New::Data::name\n";
```

> **Note**   This isn't really a nested package, at least not how it is stored by Perl. This is just two packages, and one of them just looks like it is in another package. Think of this as a technique to organize your data in a logical structure using packages.

Accessing identifiers from nested packages

> **Note**   If you have a nested package, you can't refer to identifiers of the inner package from outside of the package unless you give a fully qualified name. This includes when you attempt to access identifiers from the "outer" package:

```perl
#!perl
#nest3.pl

$name="Bob";
print "name = $name\n";

package New;
$name="Ted";

package New::Data;
$name="Fred";

package New;
print "name=$Data::name\n";   #Will not access $New::Data::name
```

use strict 'vars'

In the *Pro Perl Programming* book, the "use strict 'vars';" statement was covered. This section is a review of that topic (with some additional details as well).

use strict 'vars'

This pragma will generate an error if a variable is used that hasn't been either declared as a **my** variable or isn't fully qualified. While it is sometimes useful to have "global" variables (such as in small programs written by a single developer), "use strict 'vars'" doesn't allow this. This pragma can be very useful if you want to require **my** variables or fully qualified names.

In the following example, we are implementing "use strict 'vars'", which would cause compile errors if we didn't use fully qualified variable names:

```perl
#!perl
#use1.pl

use strict 'vars';

sub test {
    print "$main::total\n";
}

$::total=100;
my $name="Bob";
print "$name\n";
&test;
```

As you can see from the following output of use1.pl, the rules that are imposed by the pragma are followed and there are no errors:

```
[student@OCS student]$ use1.pl
Bob
100
```

Notes regarding "use strict":

- The statement **"use strict"** will enforce all restrictions (refs, subs, and vars).

- Perl built-in variables are not affected by "use strict vars".

The "use vars" pragma

As we discussed in the *Pro Perl Programming* book, you can predeclare variables by using the "use vars" pragma:

```perl
#!perl
#use2.pl
```

126

```perl
use strict 'vars';
use vars qw($total);

sub test {
    print "$total\n";
}

$total=100;
&test;
```

Output of use2.pl:

```
[student@OCS student]$ use2.pl
100
```

It's important to note that you are not declaring the variable for the life of your program. The variable is being declared only for a package ("main::" unless otherwise specified):

```perl
#!perl
#use3.pl

use strict 'vars';
use vars qw($total);

sub test {
    print "$total\n";
}

$total=100;
&test;

package Other;
print $total;
```

Note the error in the output of use3.pl which occurs when the package is switched:

```
[student@OCS student]$ use3.pl
Global symbol "$total" requires explicit package name at use3.pl line 15.
Execution of use3.pl aborted due to compilation errors.
```

use vars is obsolete

As of Perl 5.6, **use vars** is considered to be obsolete. It is covered in this book for the following reasons:

1. You may wish to write code that is backward compatible to older versions of Perl. If so, you may want to continue to use the **use vars** statement.

2. While **use vars** is considered to be obsolete, it still performs the same way that it always has. As a result, you will still see it being used in other programmer's code as well as in older scripts.

Instead of using **use vars**, you should use the **our** statement to `"globally declare"` a variable. Much like **use vars**, specifying the **our** statement will allow you to use a variable without its fully qualified name while your code has **use strict** implemented. The **our** statement will be covered in a later section of this chapter.

Identifiers not affected by packages

Almost all identifiers exist solely within the package in which they are created. Many of Perl's special identifiers, however, don't solely exist within a namespace.

Almost all of Perl's built-in variables are not affected by packages and take on an almost true global scope. For example, the default variable ($_) can be set in the main package and then accessed in another package:

```perl
#!perl
#non1.pl

$_="test";

package New;
print "$_\n";
```

In fact, the `"use strict vars;"` pragma doesn't have any effect on these sorts of Perl built-in variables:

```perl
#!perl
#non2.pl

use strict vars;

$_="test";   #Will not result in an error

package New;
print "$_\n";   #Will not result in an error
```

Note   Some of Perl's built-in variables are stored in packages. Consult the **perlvar** man page to determine which of Perl's built-in variables are not affected by packages.

Determine the current package

In some cases, you may not know the current package name. If you need to determine the current package, use the **__PACKAGE__** symbol:

```perl
$package=__PACKAGE__;
```

Example:

```perl
#!perl
#show.pl

print __PACKAGE__, "\n";

package New;
print __PACKAGE__, "\n";
```

Output of show.pl:

```
[student@OCS student]$ perl show.pl
main
New
```

Packages vs. my variables

A lot of confusion arises from the difference between package namespace and the **my** statement. Consider the following code:

```perl
#!perl
#my1.pl

$name="Bob";                 #main package variable
print "name=$name\n";        #main package variable

package New;
$name="Ted";                 #New package variable
print "name=$name\n";        #New package variable

{my $name="Nick";            #my variable
  print "name=$name\n";}     #my variable

package main;
print "name=$name\n";        #main package variable
print "name=$New::name\n";   #New package variable
```

Output of my1.pl:

```
[student@OCS student]$ perl my1.pl
name=Bob
name=Ted
name=Nick
name=Bob
name=Ted
```

Note that while the script was in the New package, we generated a block in which a **my** variable was created. Since my variables only exist for the length of the block, once we came out of the block, $name went back to being the New package's $name.

In fact, **my** variables aren't part of a package at all. Even if you declare a **my** variable in the "main scope" of your script, it isn't considered a "main" variable. Consider the following example:

```perl
#!perl
#my2.pl
```

130

```
my $name="Bob";                    #my package variable
print "name=$name\n";              #my package variable
print "name=$main::name\n";  #main package variable (not defined)
```

Output of my2.pl:

```
[student@OCS student]$ perl my2.pl
name=Bob
name=
```

In the preceding example, the variable $name in the main package is different than the $name variable in the scope of the main area of the script.

Changing to a different package doesn't affect a **my** variable either:

```
#!perl
#my3.pl

my $name="Bob";                    #my package variable
print "name=$name\n";              #my package variable
print "name=$main::name\n";  #main package variable (not defined)

package New;
print "name=$name\n";              #my package variable
$name="Ted";                       #my package variable
print "name=$name\n";              #my package variable

package main;
print "name=$name\n";              #my package variable
print "name=$main::name\n";  #main package variable (not defined)
print "name=$New::name\n";    #New package variable (not defined)
```

Output of my3.pl:

```
[student@OCS student]$ perl my3.pl
name=Bob
name=
name=Bob
name=Ted
name=Ted
name=
name=
```

In the preceding example, the variable $name is always the **my** variable. The variables $main::name and $New::name are never set because we would need to explicitly state a fully qualified name in order to do so or leave the scope in which the **my** variable was declared.

The **our** statement

On occasion, you will see a Perl script or module in which the programmer chooses to use the **our** statement instead of the **my** statement. The **our** statement often creates a lot of confusion among Perl programmers (especially novice Perl programmers).

According to the Perl man pages, the **our** statement 'has the same scoping rules as a "my" declaration, but does not create a local variable.' In a sense, an "our" variable is somewhat of a merge between a **my** variable and a variable declared with the **use vars** statement.

Remember that the **use vars** statement allowed you to specify $var instead of $Package::var and this pertained to the package itself. A **my** variable falls completely outside the realm of packages... it exists only in its own "area".

An **our** variable allows you to specify $var instead of $Package::var. So, like variables created with **use vars**, it exists inside a package. However, if you enter a new package, the **our** variable can still be accessed by specifying $var (you don't need to specify $Package::var). If you leave the scope that the our variable was created in, you need to use the fully qualified name ($Package::var) to access the variable again.

All three variable types (**use vars**, **my**, and **our**) are allowed when the use strict 'vars' pragma is in force. The example on the following page displays the differences between the three variable types:

```perl
#!perl
#our.pl

{package ABC;  #Beginning of scope and ABC package

our($our_var)="xyz";            #part of ABC package
my($my_var)="123";              #part of scope only
use vars qw($use_var);          #declares $$ABC::use_var
$use_var="abc";                 #part of ABC package
```

```perl
print "\$our_var = $our_var\n";
print "\$my_var = $my_var\n";
print "\$use_var = $use_var\n";

package New;
print "\$our_var = $our_var\n";        #Displays $ABC::our_var
print "\$my_var = $my_var\n";          #Displays "scoped" $my_var
print "\$use_var = $use_var\n";        #Doesn't exist - wrong package

}                                      #End of Scope

print "\$our_var = $our_var\n";        #Doesn't exist - out of scope & wrong
                                       #package
print "\$my_var = $my_var\n";          #Doesn't exist - out of scope
print "\$use_var = $use_var\n";        #Doesn't exist - wrong package
```

See the output of this script in the following and compare it to the statements in the our.pl program.

Output of our.pl:

```
sue% perl our.pl
$our_var = xyz
$my_var = 123
$use_var = abc
$our_var = xyz
$my_var = 123
$use_var =
$our_var =
$my_var =
$use_var =
```

Final note   The purpose of the **our** statement was to replace the **use vars** statement, not to replace the **my** statement.

133

Additional resources

In each chapter, resources are provided to provide the learner with a source for more information. These resources may include downloadable source code or links to other books or articles that will provide you more information about the topic at hand.

Resources for this chapter can be found here:

https://github.com/apress/advanced-perl-programming

Lab exercises

Modify the script you created in Chapter 6 to include the following changes:

1. Implement "use strict 'vars'".

2. Have the identifiers that are created in the subroutines that open and save the data be placed in separate packages instead of using my variables.

CHAPTER 8

Building Modules

The purpose behind Perl modules is to create code that can be loaded into another Perl script. This technique is often referred to as creating a library.

Perl modules consist of a set of related functions. By itself, a Perl module doesn't "do" anything. By calling a Perl module, your script will have access to additional functions and variables.

Some general guidelines for modules:

- The filename's extension should be ".pm".

- All identifiers in your module should be placed in a separate package (not main) to avoid the possibility of overwriting existing data.

- The filename itself (without the extension) should be the same as the package name that you define for the module.

- The package name should begin with a capital letter.

Creating a module

When you create a Perl module, you will want to take the following steps:

Step 1 – Design your module.

The most important part of this step is determining what exactly this module will do. Keep in mind that you aren't creating an entire program. A module should perform a specific task, not a group of tasks.

Step 2 – Determine what needs to be initialized.

Perl provides you with a method called a BEGIN block that allows you to execute some initialization commands. A later section will cover BEGIN blocks.

© William "Bo" Rothwell of One Course Source, Inc. 2020
W. "Bo" Rothwell, *Advanced Perl Programming*, https://doi.org/10.1007/978-1-4842-5863-7_8

Step 3 – Determine what functions will be generated.

This relates back to step #1. Your Perl module will be providing a calling program some functions. However, you probably don't want to provide all of your functions to the calling program. We will cover how to provide some of your functions to the calling program while "hiding" others in upcoming sections.

Step 4 – Determine what needs to be "cleaned up" after your module is executed.

Perl provides you with a method called an END block that allows you to execute some "clean up" commands. A later section will cover END blocks.

Step 5 – Document your module.

In order for others to understand how to use your module, you will need to provide some documentation for it. While you can use simple comments, often modules require a little more flexibility in commenting. In Chapter 10, we will cover POD, another method of documenting code that is very useful in documenting Perl modules.

BEGIN and END blocks

BEGIN and END blocks are Perl's method of allowing you a means to perform initialization statements and "clean up" statements. A BEGIN block is executed first when you call up a module, while an END block is executed after the completion of the module's code.

BEGIN blocks

BEGIN blocks are useful because they are executed as soon as Perl sees them. This means that even though the entire file hasn't been compiled yet, the BEGIN blocks are executed. The advantage behind this is that a BEGIN block can have an impact on how the program is compiled.

For example, suppose you want to add a directory location to the @INC array at the end of the array. The methods we have covered so far only allow you to add a directory to the beginning of the array. With a BEGIN block, you can add to the end of the array:

```
sub BEGIN {push (@INC, "newdirectory");}
```

Some important notes about BEGIN blocks:

- They cannot be called by you directly, only by Perl.

- While you can declare BEGIN blocks with the **sub** statement, it is optional.

- You can have multiple BEGIN blocks; they will be executed in the order that they appear in the file.

END blocks

END blocks are useful to clean up code. They will be executed after all of the program's code has been executed but prior to the interpreter exiting. The best part of END blocks is that they are executed even if a **die** function is executed in your code.

END blocks can be useful to perform actions such as deleting temporary files, saving data, and setting the $? variable.

Some important notes about END blocks:

- They cannot be called by you directly, only by Perl.

- While you can declare END blocks with the **sub** statement, it is optional.

- You can have multiple END blocks; they will be executed in the opposite order that they appear in the file.

- If your program is prematurely aborted by a signal, END block will not be executed.

Symbol tables in modules

When you create a Perl module, all work should take place in a separate package. This is because when the calling program calls your module, you don't want to overwrite identifiers that were created in the calling program.

Keep in mind that putting your identifiers in a separate package does not protect them from the calling program. If the calling program knows the package name, these identifiers can be changed.

Since you are supposed to use the same package name as your module name, knowing the package name isn't too difficult. Even if you used a package name, the programmer that is creating the calling program can always just look at your file.

In a later section, we will explore how to make "private module" identifiers.

Exporting identifiers from modules

The idea of exporting identifiers is that you want to "export" certain identifiers from your program to the calling program. In other words, even though you are in your package, you want some identifiers to be placed in the calling program's package.

In order to do this, we can use the **Exporter** module. Using the Exporter module is a three-step procedure:

```
use Exporter;
@ISA=qw(Exporter);
@EXPORT=qw(&sub1 &sub2 $var1 @array1);
```

The first line tells Perl that you want to use the Exporter module.

The second line tells Perl to use the import method to import exported identifiers.

The third line assigns the names of identifiers that you want to export to the @EXPORT array. Whatever you place inside of the @EXPORT array will be exported into the calling program.

Throughout the rest of your code, you can create variables, functions, and filehandles just like you normally would. When you finish your code, you must use the following line to avoid an error message:

```
return 1;
```

Example of a simple Perl module:

```
#MyTest.pm
package MyTest;

BEGIN {
    use Exporter();
    @ISA=qw(Exporter);
    @EXPORT=qw(&printout);
}
```

```
sub printout {print "Wow, this is cool\n";}

sub noprint {print "This shouldn't be exported!!!\n";}

return 1;
```

In this example, the printout function will be exported to the calling program. The noprint function will not be exported.

The following example calls the Perl module that was created in the preceding page:

```
#!perl
#ex1.pl

use Mytest;

&printout;
&noprint;
```

Output of ex1.pl:

```
[student@OCS student]$ ex1.pl
Wow, this is cool
Undefined subroutine &main::noprint called at ex1.pl line 8.
```

Private identifiers

In the preceding example (ex1.pl), an error occurred when trying to call the &noprint function. This is because we didn't export this function.

However, just because we don't export the function doesn't mean that it can't be called at all. In this example, we will call the noprint function:

```
#!perl
#ex2.pl

use Mytest;

&printout;
&test::noprint;
```

Output of ex2.pl:

```
[student@OCS student]$ ex2.pl
Wow, this is cool
This shouldn't be exported!!!
```

Since the package "test" is "visible" to the ex2.pl script, the function noprint can be called.

The solution to this problem and the problem of having the calling program "mess with" your module's variables is to use the **my** statement. Remember, the scope of my is "by block", not by package. If you create a **my** variable in your module, it only exists within that block (the module).

But, how does that help you out with making private functions? You can't use **my** on a function, but you can use **my** on a variable that is a reference to a function, as shown in the next example:

```
#Newtest.pm
package Newtest;

BEGIN {
    use Exporter();
    @ISA=qw(Exporter);
    @EXPORT=qw(&printout);
}

sub printout {print "Wow, this is cool\n";}

my $noprint = sub {print "This shouldn't be exported!!!\n";}

return 1;
```

Oking symbols to export from modules

Suppose you want to be able to export some identifiers, but not always export them. When you place an identifier in the @EXPORT array, Perl automatically exports all of these identifiers.

If you want to make something available to export but not have it happen automatically, place it in the @EXPORT_OK array:

```
#Testok.pm
package Testok;

BEGIN {
    use Exporter();
    @ISA=qw(Exporter);
    @EXPORT=qw(&printout);
    @EXPORT_OK=(&noprint);
}

sub printout {print "Wow, this is cool\n";}

sub noprint {print "This shouldn't be exported!!!\n";}

return 1;
```

If you want to import an identifier that is listed in the @EXPORT_OK array in the module, use this syntax:

```
use testok qw(&noprint);
```

The preceding statement can cause some problems. For example:

```
#!perl
#ex3.pl

use Testok qw(&noprint);

&printout;
&noprint;
```

While this does import the &noprint function, it no longer imports the &printout function. Once you specify what you want to import, Perl no longer automatically imports the identifiers in the @EXPORT array:

```
[student@OCS student]$ ex3.pl
Undefined subroutine &main::printout called at ex3.pl line 7.
```

This is an easy problem to solve. You can either specify all identifiers that you want imported:

```
#!perl
#ex4.pl
```

```
use Testok qw(&noprint &printout);

&printout;
&noprint;
```

Or, you can use two use statements:

```
#!perl
#ex5.pl

use Testok;
use Testok qw(&noprint);

&printout;
&noprint;
```

Module version numbers

If you update your module, you will want to keep track of different versions. The best way of doing this is to use the $VERSION variable:

```
#Testver.pm
package Testver;

BEGIN {
    use Exporter();
    @ISA=qw(Exporter);
    $VERSION=1.03;
    @EXPORT=qw(&printout);
    @EXPORT_OK=qw(&noprint);
}

sub printout {print "Wow, this is cool\n";}

sub noprint {print "This shouldn't be exported!!!\n";}

return 1;
```

Not only can the $VERSION variable be used to keep track of the version of your Perl module, it can also be used during the load process to make sure you are loading the proper version:

```perl
#!perl
#ex6.pl

use Testver 1.4;
use Testver qw(&noprint);

&printout;
&noprint;
```

Example output:

```
[student@OCS student]$ ex6.pl
Testver version 1.4 required--this is only version 1.03 at ex6.pl line 4.
BEGIN failed--compilation aborted at ex6.pl line 4.
```

use vs. require

While the **use** statement has been used throughout this course to load module, there is another statement which will load modules called **require**. There are a few subtle differences between the two statements:

- Modules loaded with **use** are loaded at compile time; modules loaded with **require** are loaded during runtime.

- **use** can be used to load pragmas; **require** can't load pragmas.

- **use** implicitly imports exported identifiers from the modules being loaded; with **require**, you have to import the identifiers yourself.

- When you use the **use** statement, you don't specify the ".pm" extension; when you use the **require** statement, you can use the ".pm" extension (or drop it if you want).

Generally, **use** is a more powerful statement and should be used in almost all cases over **require**.

A note about library files

You can "load" regular perl files into your script and use the code within your script. Using the **require** or **do** statements, you can do something like this:

```
do 'file.pl';
require 'file.pl';
```

For example, if you have this script

```
#!perl
#lib.pl

sub test {
    print "This is just a test\n";}
```

you can load it into another script like this:

```
#!perl
#load.pl

require '8_lib.pl';

&test;
```

Output of load.pl:

```
[student@OCS student]$ load.pl
This is just a test
```

So, why use the Perl module method when this simple method is available? The Perl module method is much better since it provides "checks and balances". The method listed on the previous page is rarely used anymore because of the "controls" that Perl modules provide.

If, however, you do come across a Perl script that is loading libraries the old fashion way, here are a few things you should know:

- **require** is generally preferred over **do** since it does implicit error checking (like raising an exception if it can't find the file).

- Avoid having libraries that call other libraries. This can become very ugly and difficult for the original script to understand what is going on. Perl modules and proper use of packages are much better for this.

- Old fashion Perl libraries have an extension of `.pl`, not `.pm`.

Additional resources

In each chapter, resources are provided to provide the learner with a source for more information. These resources may include downloadable source code or links to other books or articles that will provide you more information about the topic at hand.

Resources for this chapter can be found here:

```
https://github.com/apress/advanced-perl-programming
```

Online

```
http://search.cpan.org/dist/perl/pod/perlmod.pod
```

Note   Online documentation may change.

Lab exercises

Modify the program that you completed in Chapter 7 so the subroutines that open and save the data into a file are removed from the main program and put into a module. Try to make this module generic enough so you can use it to open and save any type of `"array of array"` data.

## CHAPTER 9

Installing CPAN Modules

The Comprehensive Perl Archive Network (CPAN) is a repository of Perl modules (among other Perl "things") that developers throughout the world have created. Most of the code provided on CPAN is free for any programmer's use.

Keep in mind that there is no organization that standardizes these modules. Some of the modules are very robust, but some are still in development. Before you use a module, it is best to at least look at the POD documentation, if not the code itself.

Accessing CPAN

CPAN can be accessed via a web browser by going to the following site:

`www.cpan.org/`

It can also be accessed via ftp from a number of different sites. The following graphic demonstrates just a few sites:

© William "Bo" Rothwell of One Course Source, Inc. 2020
W. "Bo" Rothwell, *Advanced Perl Programming*, https://doi.org/10.1007/978-1-4842-5863-7_9

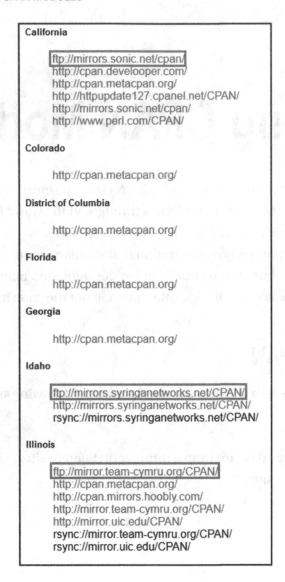

A complete list of CPAN FTP sites can be found here:

`www.cpan.org/SITES.html`

If you access CPAN from a web browser, navigation is fairly straightforward (see next section for CPAN organization). If you access CPAN via a FTP server, you will need to do a little `"hunting"` for its exact location on the server. Typically, you will find it in the `"/pub/perl/CPAN"` directory, but not always.

The following is an example of one of these FTP sites:

Index of ftp://mirrors.sonic.net/cpan/

📁 Up to higher level directory

Name	Size	Last Modified	
📁 authors		3/27/2019	11:02:00 PM
📁 clpa		8/29/2002	5:00:00 PM
CPAN.html		2/3/2010	4:00:00 PM
File: disclaimer.html	5 KB	6/30/2019	5:00:00 PM
📁 doc		4/14/2011	5:00:00 PM
File: ENDINGS	4 KB	6/30/2019	5:00:00 PM
File: index.html	9 KB	3/27/2019	11:00:00 PM
📁 indices		3/14/2011	5:00:00 PM
📁 local		10/22/2017	5:00:00 PM
ls-lR.gz		2/3/2010	4:00:00 PM
File: .message	1 KB	10/7/2003	5:00:00 PM
File: MIRRORED.BY	122 KB	12/12/2019	9:30:00 AM
File: MIRRORING.FROM	1 KB	3/27/2019	10:10:00 PM
📁 misc		3/19/2011	5:00:00 PM
📁 modules		3/27/2019	11:02:00 PM
📁 _modules		3/19/2011	5:00:00 PM
📁 ports		4/14/2011	5:00:00 PM
File: README	2 KB	2/12/1999	4:00:00 PM

While the FTP sites are very useful for things like automating the downloading of Perl modules, they are difficult to navigate until you are used to where things are. The best course of action is to get used to the website first, then tackle the FTP site.

CPAN organization

When you look at the CPAN website, you will see that there is a lot going on. It does change a bit over time as well, but as of the writing of this book, it looks like the following:

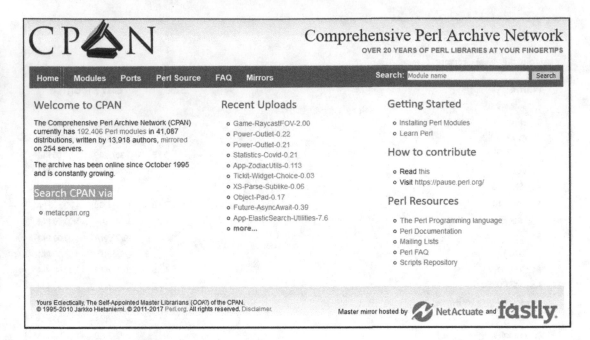

CPAN's website is organized into many different sections. The following list provides a brief description of each of these sections.

The menu bar

The options in the menu bar include

- **Home** – To bring you back to the home page when you move to another page.

- **Modules** – This takes you to a section in which you can learn how to install modules, find modules, and contribute your own modules (more on this option when we discuss searching for modules later in this section).

- **Ports** – A list of platforms that Perl is supported on. Very useful if you have a nonstandard operating system that you want to use Perl on.

- **Perl Source** – Demonstrates how to get access to the Perl source code.

- **FAQ** – Very useful Frequently Asked Questions.

- **Mirrors** – Different sites that host CPAN.

- **Search** – One way that you can search for Perl modules.

The main page

Not every section of the main page will be described here, but here are some of the highlights:

- **Welcome to CPAN** – Take a look at how many Perl modules are available!

- **Search CPAN via** – This category includes links that allow you to search for Perl modules using a tool called Metaspan (more on this in a later section).

- **Getting Started** – A nice introduction to installing modules and learning Perl.

- **Perl Resources** – Additional useful sources of Perl information.

Searching for modules

There are a few different techniques for searching for modules. This section describes these techniques and discusses some of the pros and cons of each.

To start with, you can use the Search: feature on the menu bar. For example, suppose we want to search for a module that allowed us to access data in an Excel file. We could do the following search:

The results of this search are shown in the following:

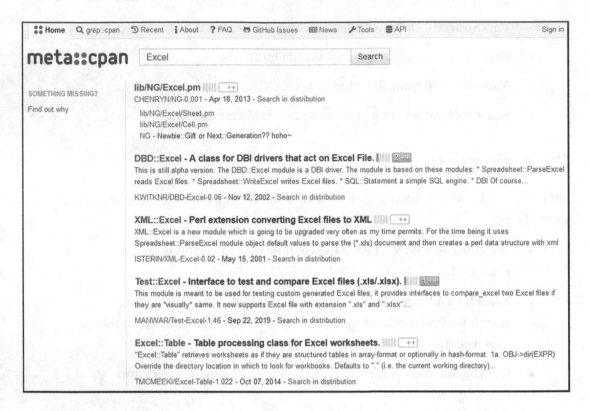

Note that the search engine that was used is the `meta::cpan` tool (recall there was a link to this on the main page). This tool is useful, but even more useful can be the `grep::cpan` tool (note the link to this at the top of the `meta::cpan` results page). With `grep::cpan`, you can use regular expressions:

For example, you could search for [eE]xcel by entering this in the "search with Perl Compatible RegEx" box. Note: This doesn't just search the module names like meta::cpan; it searches all of the descriptions as well. Results may take a while and might include a bunch of modules that you are not interested in.

Note   If you click "Modules" from the main menu bar, you will see a section named "How to find modules". Under that section, there is a "Browse" section, where you can list all of the modules (or authors, categories, etc.). Given that there are almost 200,000 modules, using the browse technique to search for modules is not recommended.

I found a good module, now what?

Suppose you find a good module that you want to use, like the following:

XML::Excel - Perl extension converting Excel files to XML ‖‖‖ `( ++ )`

XML::Excel is a new module which is going to be upgraded very often as my time permits. For the time being it uses Spreadsheet::ParseExcel module object default values to parse the (*.xls) document and then creates a perl data structure with xml

ISTERIN/XML-Excel-0.02 - May 15, 2001 - Search in distribution

---

Your first thought might be to download and install it. Think again before you do this. Consider that you may end up putting a lot of work into using this module only to discover it doesn't fit your needs. Some considerations when picking a module:

1. **How old is the module?** Look more closely to that XML::Excel module. The date on it is May 15, 2001. Both XML and Excel have changed since 2001, so this might not be a good choice.

2. **How good is the documentation?** Click the module name and read the documentation. If it looks very vague, maybe this isn't the right module for you.

3. **Is the author approachable?** Here is a good trick: if you are considering using a module and want to know if the author is willing to answer questions, before you use the module, send the author an email like this: "Hi, I'm thinking about using

your YYY:ZZZ module for a project that I'm working on.
<briefly describe project here> Do you think this would
be a good fit and do you have any suggestions?" If you
don't get any response, you probably won't get a response if you
run into problems.

4. **Is the source code understandable to me?** Go ahead and
   download the source code (you can do that on the module details
   page) and take a look at it. Does it make sense enough so you
   could debug any problems that might arise? If not, maybe another
   module would make more sense.

You can probably think of more considerations (like what license the code is under).
The point is to not just blindly download and use modules. Think about it very carefully
and explore the module as much as you reasonably can. This will save you a large
amount of time and headaches in the future.

Installing a CPAN module manually

If you are on a UNIX or Linux system, you may have to install your new module
manually. This would include the following steps:

1. Downloading the Perl module

2. Possibility uncompressing and untaring the file

3. Reviewing the "readme" or "install" file that came with the
   module to see if there are any custom instructions

4. Running the command "perl Makefile.pl"

5. Modifying the "make" file to include system information for your
   system (e.g., the location of your c compiler)

6. Running the **make** command

7. Running the **make test** command

8. Running the **make install** command

On a Windows system, it would be even more complex as some of the tools that you need aren't installed on Windows by default. Consider installing a module manually to be your last resort. Try the other methods discussed in this chapter first.

Installing CPAN modules using the CPAN module

The manual method of installing Perl modules can be a real pain. An easier method is the CPAN module. To start the interactive CPAN shell, run the following command:

`perl -MCPAN -e shell`

Example on a Windows system running Strawberry Perl:

```
C:\Windows\System32>perl -MCPAN -e shell
Unable to get Terminal Size. The Win32 GetConsoleScreenBufferInfo call didn't work. The COLUMNS and LINES environment va
riables didn't work. at C:\Strawberry\perl\vendor\lib\Term\ReadLine\readline.pm line 410.

cpan shell -- CPAN exploration and modules installation (v2.27)
Enter 'h' for help.

cpan>
```

Note   The first time you use the CPAN module, it will prompt you for information that it needs to automatically install modules. In most cases, you should be able to accept the default answers. In others, however, you may need to find some information.

Listing available commands

To list the commands that are available in CPAN, use the **help** command:

```
cpan> help

Display Information                                               (ver 2.27)
 command   argument          description
 a,b,d,m   WORD or /REGEXP/  about authors, bundles, distributions, modules
 i         WORD or /REGEXP/  about any of the above
 ls        AUTHOR or GLOB    about files in the author's directory
    (with WORD being a module, bundle or author name or a distribution
    name of the form AUTHOR/DISTRIBUTION)

Download, Test, Make, Install...
 get       download                  clean    make clean
 make      make (implies get)        look     open subshell in dist directory
 test      make test (implies make)  readme   display these README files
 install   make install (implies test)  perldoc  display POD documentation

Upgrade installed modules
 r         WORDs or /REGEXP/ or NONE    report updates for some/matching/all
 upgrade   WORDs or /REGEXP/ or NONE    upgrade some/matching/all modules

Pragmas
 force  CMD    try hard to do command  fforce CMD    try harder
 notest CMD    skip testing

Other
 h,?            display this menu       ! perl-code    eval a perl command
 o conf [opt]   set and query options   q              quit the cpan shell
 reload cpan    load CPAN.pm again      reload index   load newer indices
 autobundle     Snapshot                recent         latest CPAN uploads
```

Note   There are many commands available. The focus of this chapter is to install
CPAN modules, so the commands covered have to do with installing. Feel free to
try some of the commands that aren't covered in this chapter.

Listing available modules

To list the modules that are available, use the **i** command. Note: This command could
end up taking a long time to run (remember, there are almost 200,000 modules). It would
be best to know the name of your module prior to using the cpan module to avoid delays
in installing:

```
cpan> i
output omitted
```

Installing modules

To install a module, use the **install** command:

```
cpan> install Tie::IxHash
Fetching with LWP:
http://cpan.strawberryperl.com/authors/01mailrc.txt.gz
Fetching with LWP:
http://cpan.strawberryperl.com/modules/02packages.details.txt.gz
Fetching with LWP:
http://cpan.strawberryperl.com/modules/03modlist.data.gz
Creating database file ... Done!
Running install for module 'Tie::IxHash'
Fetching with LWP:
http://cpan.strawberryperl.com/authors/id/C/CH/CHORNY/Tie-IxHash-1.23.tar.gz
Fetching with LWP:
http://cpan.strawberryperl.com/authors/id/C/CH/CHORNY/CHECKSUMS
Checksum for C:\STRAWB~1\cpan\sources\authors\id\C\CH\CHORNY\Tie-
IxHash-1.23.tar.gz ok
Scanning cache C:\STRAWB~1\cpan\build for sizes
DONE
Configuring C/CH/CHORNY/Tie-IxHash-1.23.tar.gz with Build.PL
Created MYMETA.yml and MYMETA.json
Creating new 'Build' script for 'Tie-IxHash' version '1.23'
  CHORNY/Tie-IxHash-1.23.tar.gz
  C:\Strawberry\perl\bin\perl.exe Build.PL -- OK
Running Build for C/CH/CHORNY/Tie-IxHash-1.23.tar.gz
Building Tie-IxHash
  CHORNY/Tie-IxHash-1.23.tar.gz
  C:\Strawberry\perl\bin\perl.exe ./Build -- OK
Running Build test for CHORNY/Tie-IxHash-1.23.tar.gz
t\each-delete.t .. ok
t\ixhash.t ....... ok
t\pod.t .......... ok
All tests successful.
Files=3, Tests=29,  1 wallclock secs ( 0.06 usr +  0.00 sys =  0.06 CPU)
```

```
Result: PASS
Lockfile removed.
  CHORNY/Tie-IxHash-1.23.tar.gz
  C:\Strawberry\perl\bin\perl.exe ./Build test -- OK
Running Build install for CHORNY/Tie-IxHash-1.23.tar.gz
Building Tie-IxHash
Installing C:\STRAWB~1\perl\site\lib\Tie\IxHash.pm
  CHORNY/Tie-IxHash-1.23.tar.gz
  C:\Strawberry\perl\bin\perl.exe ./Build install --uninst 1 -- OK
```

Note   When you are finished installing the module, you can quit the cpan module by using the quit command:

cpan> **quit**

Lockfile removed.

Using the Perl Package Manager to install modules

The Perl Package Manager (ppm) is a great tool for automatically installing modules. This tool works on ActiveState's version of Perl. ActiveState's Perl is currently available on Windows-based OS, Linux, and Solaris.

Please note the following statement from ActiveState's website:

> **NOTE**: PPM is being phased out as ActiveState moves forward with a new and improved solution for Perl package management across all platforms. While PPM has been included in all versions of ActivePerl up to and including version 5.26, the number of modules with which it worked has steadily declined. As a result, starting with ActivePerl 5.28, PPM modules are no longer available.
>
> That doesn't mean that you're out in the cold when it comes to installing Perl modules. Until ActiveState fully rolls out its new solution, you can (as always) use CPAN to install any additional modules you require into your ActivePerl runtime.

This is a very recent change and should only be an issue if you are using ActivePerl 5.28 or higher. The following discussion is only for ActivePerl 5.26 and previous.

Starting ppm

To start ppm, just type **ppm**:

```
# ppm
```

This will take you into an interactive GUI-based program:

Note   On some systems, the ppm command may take you into a command-line only session. To start the GUI-based program, you may need to execute the following command:

```
ppm gui
```

Displaying packages

By default, only installed packages are displayed. To display all packages, installed and available to install, click View ➤ All Packages:

Installed packages have a gold-colored icon next to them, and available packages have a gray-colored icon.

Accessing repositories

Unless you purchased the commercial distribution of Perl from ActiveState, you will get an error message when trying to install new packages. The only available packages displayed by default come from the ActiveState repository:

Package Name	Area	Installed	Repo ▲	Available	Abstract
CVS-Metrics			ActiveState Package ...	0.18	Utilities for proc...
CaCORE			ActiveState Package ...	3.2.1_r1	
Cache-Adaptive			ActiveState Package ...	0.03	A Cache Engine...
Cache-Against...			ActiveState Package ...	1.016	Cache data stru...
Cache-Bench...			ActiveState Package ...	0.011	Tests the qualit...
Cache-Bounded			ActiveState Package ...	v1.06	A size-aware in...
Cache-Cache			ActiveState Package ...	1.06	the Cache interf...
Cache-CacheF...			ActiveState Package ...	1.10	Factory class fo...
Cache-Cascade			ActiveState Package ...	0.05	Get/set values t...
Cache-Ehcache			ActiveState Package ...	0.03	client library for...
Cache-FastMe...			ActiveState Package ...	0.01	In-memory cac...
Cache-FastM...			ActiveState Package ...	1.39	Uses an mmap'...
Cache-FastM...			ActiveState Package ...	1.28.1	Uses an mmap'...
Cache-Funky			ActiveState Package ...	0.06	How is simple, ...
Cache-Funky-...			ActiveState Package ...	0.07	Cache::Funky ...
Cache-KyotoT...			ActiveState Package ...	0.12	KyotoTycoon cli...
Cache-LRU			ActiveState Package ...	0.03	a simple, fast i...
Cache-Memca...			ActiveState Package ...	1.24	client library for...

Attempting to install one of these packages on a community release of ActiveState Perl will result in the following error message:

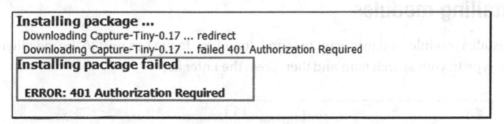

If you are using an older version of Perl, you will also find that the modules will be out of date. For example, the Capture-Tiny package listed earlier was version 0.17 when the latest version at the time of this writing was 0.24.

Fortunately, many of these packages are available from other (third-party) repositories. To access these, first click Edit ➤ Preferences:

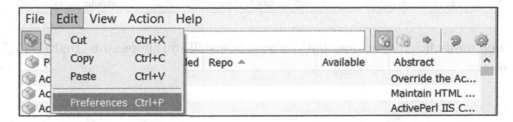

Next, click the Repositories tab. While you can insert the location of custom repositories, there is also a list of common repositories available next to "Suggested":

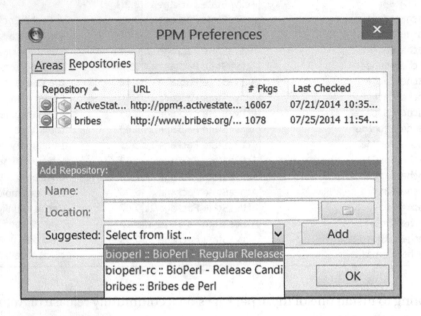

Installing modules

To install a module, you may want to search for it first. In the box next to the magnifying glass, type in your search term and then press the Enter key:

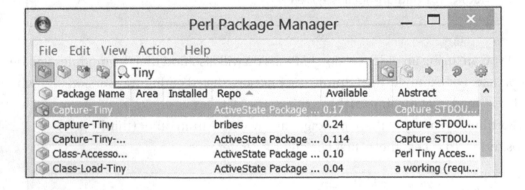

Then right-click the package that you want to install and choose the "Install..." option:

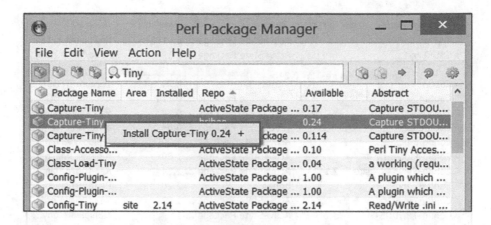

The package is now marked to install. Select any additional packages that you want to install and then click File ➤ Run Marked Actions:

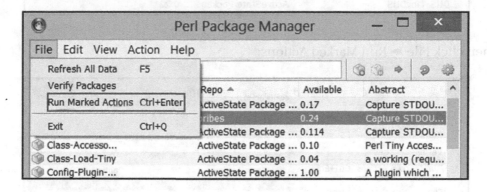

Watch the bottom of the window for the results:

```
Installing package ...
  Downloading Capture-Tiny-0.24 ... done
  Unpacking Capture-Tiny-0.24 ... done
  Generating HTML for Capture-Tiny-0.24 ... done
  Updating files in site area ... done
Installing package done
```

Deleting packages

To delete a package, first right-click the package name and then click the "Remove..." option:

Package Name	Area	Installed	Repo ▲		Available	Abstract
App-ZofCMS-P...			ActiveState Package ...		0.0102	tiny plugin to fe...
CSS-Tiny			ActiveState Package ...		1.19	Read/Write .css...
Captur...		Remove Capture-Tiny 0.24	-	e Package ... 0.17		Capture STDOU...
Captur...					0.24	Capture STDOU...
Captur...		Install Capture-Tiny 0.17	+	e Package ... 0.114		Capture STDOU...
Class-...				e Package ... 0.10		Perl Tiny Acces...
Class-L...		Verify Capture-Tiny 0.24		e Package ... 0.04		a working (requ...
Config-Plugin-...			ActiveState Package ...		1.00	A plugin which ...
Config-Plugin-...			ActiveState Package ...		1.00	A plugin which ...
Config-Tiny	site	2.14	ActiveState Package ...		2.14	Read/Write .ini ...
Config-Tiny			bribes		2.20	Read/Write .ini ...
Config-Tiny-Or...			ActiveState Package ...		1.02	Read/Write ord...
Config-TinyDNS			ActiveState Package ...		1	Manipulate tiny...
Config-YAML-...			ActiveState Package ...		1.42.0	simple reading ...
Crypt-TEA			ActiveState Package ...		1.25	Tiny Encryption ...
Crypt-Tea			ActiveState Package ...		2.12	Tiny Encryption ...
Crypt-Tea_JS			ActiveState Package ...		2.23	The New Tiny E...
DNS-TinyDNS			ActiveState Package ...		0.22	

Then click File ➤ Run Marked Actions:

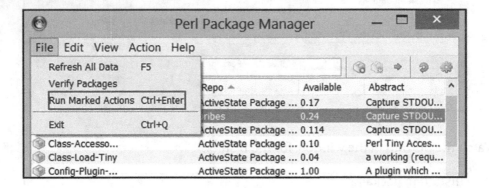

Watch the bottom of the window for the results:

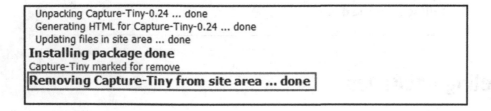

Listing what modules are currently installed

The easiest way to list what Perl modules are currently installed is to use view the perllocal.pod file. This file is updated whenever a module is installed on the system.

The location of this file can vary from platform to platform. Typically on UNIX-based systems, this file is located in /usr/local/lib/perl5/*version_num/arch*, while on a Windows-based system, it is located in c:/Perl/lib. There really is no set location for this file, so perform a search for the perllocal.pod file.

Since this is a POD formatted document, you will need to use the **perldoc** utility to view it:

```
[student@linux1 student]$ perldoc perllocal.pod
User Contributed Perl Documentation                    PERLLOCAL(1)
    Thu Mar  1 16:29:35 2001: Module the Tk manpage

    o    installed into: /usr/local/lib/perl5/site_perl/5.005
{remaining output omitted}
```

An example on a Windows system with an ActivePerl installation:

```
C:\Users\bo\Documents\Unzipped\ActivePerl-5.8.6.811-MSWin32-x86-122208\ActivePerl-5.8.6.811\Perl\lib>perldoc perllocal.p
od
  Mon Dec 13 10:24:28 2004: "Module" ActiveState::RelocateTree
    *    "installed into:
         C:\TEMP\perl-----------------------------------------please-run-t
         he-install-script------------------------------------------\site\li
         b"

    *    "LINKTYPE: dynamic"

    *    "VERSION: 0.03"

    *    "EXE_FILES: bin/reloc_perl"

  Mon Dec 13 10:24:40 2004: "Module" Compress::Zlib
    *    "installed into:
         C:\TEMP\perl----------------------------------- ------please-run-t
         he-install-script------------------------------------------\site\li
         b"

    *    "LINKTYPE: dynamic"

    *    "VERSION: 1.33"
```

Note   We will cover the **perldoc** utility in detail in Chapter 10.

Additional resources

Books

In each chapter, resources are provided to provide the learner with a source for more information. These resources may include downloadable source code or links to other books or articles that will provide you more information about the topic at hand.

Resources for this chapter can be found here:

```
https://github.com/apress/advanced-perl-programming
```

Online

```
http://search.cpan.org/dist/perl/pod/perlmodinstall.pod
```

Note   Online documentation may change.

Lab exercises

No exercises for this chapter.

CHAPTER 10

POD

POD (Plain Old Documentation) is the method you want to use to document your Perl modules. While simple comments work well for pointing out tricky code, they are cumbersome when you want to give a detailed explanation of your module.

POD was designed so you can create formatted comments. POD uses tags to specify text formats such as fonts as well as text positions.

POD can be embedded within your code or placed in a separate file. When embedded within your code, there are methods of telling the Perl interpreter when to execute code and when to skip over lines.

You put POD documentation together in paragraph format. Each POD paragraph is separated by a blank line. There are three types of paragraphs in POD:

- **Command** – A command paragraph is used to treat a chunk of text is a certain fashion. For example, you can use a Command paragraph to generate a list.

- **Text (or ordinary)** – A text or ordinary paragraph is used to generate text that can either be formatted (bold, italic, hyperlink) or just plain text. A markup feature, similar to HTML or XML, is used to specify formatting.

- **Verbatim** – A verbatim paragraph is used to generate text that contains no formatting. Anything in a verbatim paragraph is considered "plain text."

POD commands

POD commands begin with the equal sign and are immediately followed by the command. Text can follow the command as well. The end of the line is the end of the command.

© William "Bo" Rothwell of One Course Source, Inc. 2020
W. "Bo" Rothwell, *Advanced Perl Programming*, https://doi.org/10.1007/978-1-4842-5863-7_10

The following is a summary of the POD commands that are available:

POD command	Meaning
=back	Used in conjunction with =over and =item to generate a list
=begin *format*	Allows you to specify text to be interpreted by a different parser such as HTML
=cut	Used to specify the end of POD text
=end	Ends a =begin block
=for *format*	Specifies a format change that will affect the next paragraph only
=head1 *text*	Specifies that the following text is formatted by the predefined "head1" format
=head2	Specifies that the following text is formatted by the predefined "head2" format
=item	Used in conjunction with =over and =back to generate a list
=over	Used in conjunction with =back and =item to generate a list
=pod	Specifies the beginning of POD text

Using headings

The POD commands **=head1**, **=head2**, **=head3**, and **=head4** provide predefined formats. These are primarily designed to create an indented style format for documentation. The following code describes how they are used:

#head.pod

=head1   This is head1

Text under head1

=head2   This is head2

Text under head2

=head3   This is head3

Text under head3

=head4   This is head4

Text under head4

How these are displayed really depends on the POD interpreter that is used. Some POD interpreters, such as the **perldoc** command (this command will be covered in more detail later in this Chapter), may consider **=head2**, **=head3**, and **=head4** to be the same or very similar. For example, perldoc indents the head values differently as shown in the following output but doesn't display them in different fonts or font sizes:

```
[student@OCS student]$ perldoc head.pod
```

```
This is head1
    Text under head1

  This is head2
    Text under head2

  This is head3
    Text under head3

  This is head4
    Text under head4
```

Starting and ending POD text

When you embed POD within a Perl script, you need to tell the Perl interpreter when to stop "looking at" the code. The **=pod** command tells Perl to stop interpreting code. The **=cut** tells Perl to start interpreting code again.

The **=pod** command is rarely used because any POD command (except **=cut**) will "turn on" POD. However, if you want to start POD documentation with a verbatim paragraph, then **=pod** would be necessary.

When POD is "on," the Perl interpreter will ignore everything until POD is "turned off." POD interpreters, which will be discussed later, will ignore Perl code and only parse POD Commands.

Using other formats

Instead of using POD formats, you can specify other formats. Additional formats that POD can handle are "html," "text," "man," "latex," "tex," and "roff." If you already know how to format text in these other formats, this can be a useful option.

To "turn on" a different format for a single paragraph, use the **=for** command:

```
=for text
```

To "turn on" a different format for a block, use the **=begin** command to start the block and **=end** to stop the block:

```
=begin text
This is plain text
=end text
```

Using POD to create multi-line comments

A common question people have when learning Perl is "does Perl support multi-line comments like some other languages, like C++, offer?" Typically, novice Perl programmers are told "no," but in reality multi-line comments are possible by using POD.

Recall that any POD commands or text will not be interpreted by the Perl interpreter. So, you could create a multi-line comment by doing the following:

```
=for text

    This is a comment
    It can span multiple lines

=cut
```

However, the problem with this technique is if you are actually using POD in this program to create documentation, then the multi-line comment will be included with the POD output.

To avoid this, use the following:

```
=for comment
```

Anything between this command and **=cut** will be ignored by both the Perl interpreter and any POD interpreter. You can even omit the extra blank lines after **=for** and before **=cut** in this specific case.

Creating a list

You can create an indented numbered or bulleted list with POD. To do this, you need to use three commands:

=over	This command tells POD to begin a list. You can specify a numeric value to indicate how many "spaces" to use to intend (e.g., =over 4).
=item	This command tells POD to add an item to the list. To specify bulleted lists, use this syntax: "=item *". To specify numbered lists, use this syntax: "=item 1.", "=item 2.", etc.
=back	This command tells POD to stop the list.

The following example demonstrates a simple two-item list:

```
=over 4

=item *
This is one item

=item *
This is another item

=back
```

The following demonstrates how the pod list would appear:

```
[student@OCS student]$ perldoc podlist.pod
    *    This is one item

    *    This is another item
```

POD text

POD text can be displayed as "plain text" or formatted using the following commands:

Text command	Meaning
I<text>	Italicize text
B<text>	Bold text
S<text>	Nonbreaking spaces text
C<code>	Display "code" in a typewriter font to distinguish from other text
L<name>	A link to either another document or a section in this document
E<lt>	A less than character: "<"
E<gt>	A greater than character: ">"
E<sol>	A slash character: "\"
E<verbar>	A pipe character: "|"

Notes:

- Look at the *perlpod* man page for additional text commands.

- Depending on your POD interpreter, some of the preceding commands may not result in any text change. For example, the perldoc command typically ignores these options as the output is normally in a terminal window:

```
[student@OCS student]$ perldoc podformat.pod
     This is very important - please report all data to Frank.
```

POD verbatim

If you don't want any formatting done on your text, you can use the verbatim method. With the verbatim method, no "special" characters are allowed (like italics, bold, etc.).

If you don't want to have formatted text, you can use verbatim text by indenting your text with at least one space:

This is an example

The primary purpose of POD verbatim is when you want to use a character that is normally considered a formatting character. For example, consider the following:

=for text

To display in bold, use B<text>

A POD interpreter might attempt to make "text" bold when it displays this line. If you don't want the code to be interpreted, but rather display just as it appears, just put a space in front of the line:

```
=for text
```

```
To display in bold, use B<text>
```

POD examples

In the following example, we have a file that only contains POD commands:

```
#pod1.pod
=head1 EXAMPLE
```

```
An example of POD
```

```
=head2 DESCRIPTION
```

```
This is an example of how bulleted lists work:
=over 4
```

```
=item *
```

```
Item one
```

```
=item *
```

```
Item two
```

```
=back
```

```
We are still displaying text under the head2 command here
```

```
Here is an example of numbered lists
```

```
=over 4
```

```
=item 1.
```

```
Item one
```

```
=item 2.
```

Item two

=back

One last thing: This is an example of verbatim text:

 A \ is just a slash, a < is just a less than sign...

The following demonstrates the output of pod1.pl:

```
[student@OCS student]$ perldoc pod1.pod
EXAMPLE
    An example of POD

DESCRIPTION
    This is an example of how bulleted lists work:

      •  Item one

      •  Item two

    We are still displaying text under the head2 command here

    Here is an example of numbered lists

      1. Item one

      2. Item two

    One last thing: This is an example of verbatim text:

    A \ is just a slash, a < is just a less than sign...
```

In this example, POD is embedded in a Perl script:

```
#!perl
#pod2.pl

=head1 EXAMPLE

Just an example of POD within a perl script...easy, isn't it?

=cut

sub hello {
```

```
    print "hello\n"
}

&hello;
```

Note that pod2.pl can be run as a normal Perl script. The POD documentation has no impact on the execution of the script:

```
[student@OCS student]$ perl pod2.pl
hello
```

You can also view the POD documentation of the pod2.pl script:

```
[student@OCS student]$ perldoc pod2.pl
EXAMPLE
    Just an example of POD within a perl script...easy, isn't it?
```

Note   While you will sometimes see POD documentation in a separate file, it is much more common to see it in the script itself. Typically, it appears at the top of the script, but you will sometimes see it at the bottom as well. There aren't any rules as to where you place POD documentation.

Common POD problems

As you can probably tell, POD is very simple. It's not very fancy, but to create "Plain Old Documentation," quickly and easily, it works very well.

Because it is so simple, very few things can go wrong. Here is a list of the major potential problems:

1. Forgetting to use **=pod** to begin (or **=cut** to end) when you embed POD in Perl scripts.

2. Some POD interpreters require blank lines between commands and the text that follows.

3. Not understanding the "text commands." For example, some POD interpreters add additional text when you use the **L<link>** command.

POD utilities

There are several utilities that are useful when you work with POD.

Note   Not all of these utilities may be available on your system.

---

podchecker

This utility is useful to check the syntax of your POD file. If there are no syntax errors, podchecker reports "syntax OK":

[student@OCS student]$ **podchecker pod1.txt**
pod1.pod pod syntax OK.

Based on the current documentation, **podchecker** will check the following (note: this list hasn't changed for a very long time, so expect this will be the same check for future Perl 5 releases):

> - Unknown '=xxxx' commands, unknown 'X<...>' interior-sequences, and unterminated interior sequences.
>
> - Check for proper balancing of `=begin` and `=end` . The contents of such a block are generally ignored, i.e. no syntax checks are performed.
>
> - Check for proper nesting and balancing of `=over` , `=item` and `=back` .
>
> - Check for same nested interior-sequences (e.g. `L<...L<...>...>`).
>
> - Check for malformed or non-existing entities `E<...>` .
>
> - Check for correct syntax of hyperlinks `L<...>` . See perlpod for details.
>
> - Check for unresolved document-internal links. This check may also reveal misspelled links that seem to be internal links but should be links to something else.

If there are any syntax problems, POD indicates what the problems are:

[student@OCS student]$ **podchecker pod3.txt**
*** ERROR: empty =head1 at line 3 in file pod3.txt*
pod3.txt has 1 pod syntax error.

perldoc

The **perldoc** command will display the output of a POD file:

```
[student@OCS student]$ perldoc pod2.pl
EXAMPLE
    Just an example of POD within a perl script...easy, isn't it?
```

In addition to modules, the Perl core documentation is also in POD format. To see the core Perl documentation, use the following command:

```
[student@OCS student]$ perldoc perl
NAME
    perl - The Perl 5 language interpreter

SYNOPSIS
    perl [ -sTtuUWX ] [ -hv ] [ -V[:*configvar*] ]
    [ -cw ] [ -d[t][:*debugger*] ] [ -D[*number/list*] ]
    [ -pna ] [ -F*pattern* ] [ -l[*octal*] ] [ -0[*octal/hexadecimal*] ]
    [ -I*dir* ] [ -m[-]*module* ] [ -M[-]*'module...'* ] [ -f ]
    [ -C [*number/list*] ] [ -S ] [ -x[*dir*] ] [ -i[*extension*] ]
    [ [-e|-E] *'command'* ] [ -- ] [ *programfile* ] [ *argument* ]...

    For more information on these options, you can run "perldoc perlrun".

GETTING HELP
    The perldoc program gives you access to all the documentation that
    comes with Perl. You can get more documentation, tutorials and
    community support online at <http://www.perl.org/>.
{remaining output omitted}
```

Included in the output of the preceding command is a list of other documents that you can view, such as the following:

```
[student@OCS student]$ perldoc perlcheat
NAME
    perlcheat - Perl 5 Cheat Sheet
```

DESCRIPTION
    This 'cheat sheet' is a handy reference, meant for beginning Perl
    programmers. Not everything is mentioned, but 195 features may already
    be overwhelming.
{remaining output omitted}

If you read through the main perldoc documentation, you will see a bunch of FAQs. The **-q** option to perldoc allows you to search the FAQs using a keyword:

```
[student@OCS student]$ perldoc -q sort
Found in /usr/bin/perl/lib/pods/perlfaq4.pod
  How do I sort an array by (anything)?
    Supply a comparison function to sort() (described in "sort" in
    perlfunc):

        @list = sort { $a <=> $b } @list;

    The default sort function is cmp, string comparison, which would sort
    "(1, 2, 10)" into "(1, 10, 2)". "<=>", used above, is the numerical
    comparison operator.
{remaining output omitted}
```

Note that the output of the **perldoc -q sort** command also showed you where the POD file exists (/usr/bin/perl/lib/pods/perlfaq4.pod in the previous example). This location can vary based on your platform (operating system) and type of Perl that you installed (standard, Strawberry, ActiveState, etc.). The advantage of knowing this location is you can go look at a large collection of POD files as a way of learning POD better.

If you want to see a list of all of Perl's functions, view the **perlfunc** document. This is also an excellent way to see a list of what functions are available on the version of Perl that you are currently using:

```
[student@OCS student]$ perldoc perlfunc
NAME
    perlfunc - Perl builtin functions
```

DESCRIPTION

The functions in this section can serve as terms in an expression. They fall into two major categories: list operators and named unary operators. These differ in their precedence relationship with a following comma. (See the precedence table in perlop.) List operators take more than one argument, while unary operators can never take more than one argument. Thus, a comma terminates the argument of a unary operator, but merely separates the arguments of a list operator. A unary operator generally provides scalar context to its argument, while a list operator may provide either scalar or list contexts for its arguments. If it does both, scalar arguments come first and list argument follow, and there can only ever be one such list argument. For instance, "splice" has three scalar arguments followed by a list, whereas "gethostbyname" has four scalar arguments.

{skipping output…}

Input and output functions

    "binmode", "close", "closedir", "dbmclose", "dbmopen", "die", "eof", "fileno", "flock", "format", "getc", "print", "printf", "read", "readdir", "readline", "rewinddir", "say", "seek", "seekdir", "select", "syscall", "sysread", "sysseek", "syswrite", "tell", "telldir", "truncate", "warn", "write"

{remaining output omitted}

Being able to view the list of functions can be helpful in many ways. For example, suppose you forget the name of a function that you rarely use. You could read through the list of functions, or, if your platform has a filter command like the **grep** command, you could send the output to the filter command to view just the lines you want to see.

To see a specific function's documentation, use the **-f** option:

[student@OCS student]$ **perldoc -f sort**

    sort SUBNAME LIST

    sort BLOCK LIST

    sort LIST

        In list context, this sorts the LIST and returns the sorted list value. In scalar context, the behaviour of "sort" is undefined.

If SUBNAME or BLOCK is omitted, "sort"s in standard string
comparison order. If SUBNAME is specified, it gives the name of
a subroutine that returns an integer less than, equal to, or
greater than 0, depending on how the elements of the list are to
be ordered. (The "<=>" and "cmp" operators are extremely useful
in such routines.) SUBNAME may be a scalar variable name
(unsubscripted), in which case the value provides the name of
(or a reference to) the actual subroutine to use. In place of a
SUBNAME, you can provide a BLOCK as an anonymous, in-line
sort subroutine.

{remaining output omitted}

If you want to see a module documentation, use the following syntax:

```
[student@OCS student]$ perldoc File::Copy
NAME
    File::Copy - Copy files or filehandles

SYNOPSIS
        use File::Copy;

        copy("sourcefile","destinationfile") or die "Copy failed: $!";
        copy("Copy.pm",\*STDOUT);
        move("/dev1/sourcefile","/dev2/destinationfile");

        use File::Copy "cp";

        $n = FileHandle->new("/a/file","r");
        cp($n,"x");

DESCRIPTION
    The File::Copy module provides two basic functions, "copy" and "move",
    which are useful for getting the contents of a file from one place to
    another.
```

{remaining output omitted}

You can even have **perldoc** tell you where the module is installed by using the **-l**
option. This can be useful when you want to view the module code directly:

```
[student@OCS student]$ perldoc -l File::Copy
C:\Perl64\lib\File\Copy.pm
```

Or, to see the raw code of a module, use the **-m** option:

```
[student@OCS student]$ perldoc -m File::Copy
# File/Copy.pm. Written in 1994 by Aaron Sherman <ajs@ajs.com>. This
# source code has been placed in the public domain by the author.
# Please be kind and preserve the documentation.
#
# Additions copyright 1996 by Charles Bailey.  Permission is granted
# to distribute the revised code under the same terms as Perl itself.
package File::Copy;

use 5.006;
use strict;
use warnings; no warnings 'newline';
use File::Spec;
use Config;
# During perl build, we need File::Copy but Scalar::Util might not be built
# yet.  And then we need these games to avoid loading overload, as that
# will confuse miniperl during the bootstrap of perl.
my $Scalar_Util_loaded = eval q{ require Scalar::Util; require overload; 1 };
# We want HiRes stat and utime if available
BEGIN { eval q{ use Time::HiRes qw( stat utime ) } };
our(@ISA, @EXPORT, @EXPORT_OK, $VERSION, $Too_Big, $Syscopy_is_copy);
sub copy;
sub syscopy;
{remaining output omitted}
```

Additional utilities

Depending on factors such as your platform and version of Perl, you might also have access to the following POD utilities:

> **pod2fm** – Translates POD files to FrameMaker formats
>
> **pod2html** – Translates POD files to HTML format
>
> **pod2latex** – Translates POD files to LaTeX format
>
> **pod2man** – Translates POD files to man page format
>
> **pod2text** – Translates POD files to text format

POD style

When creating POD documentation, there are several things that you may want to consider. For some Perl programmers, one of the most important things to consider is where to place your POD documentation.

To begin with, in most cases your POD documentation should be embedded within your Perl module file and not in a separate file. Placing POD in a separate file poses problems when the module is copied to another location (and the POD file is not).

When you place the POD documentation in your Perl module, you basically have three choices:

1. **At the top of your module file** – Several Perl programmers take this approach; however, this does tend to frustrate other programmers who view the module file directly as they don't want to have to scroll through a bunch of POD documentation to read the actual code.

2. **Spaced throughout the module file** – Some Perl programmers use this technique to provide documentation while also commenting sections of the Perl code. However, it does tend to make reading the code directly difficult.

3. **At the end of your module file** – Because other programmers rarely read POD directly from your file, this may be the best option. Place all of the Perl code first and POD at the end of the code.

For other POD style considerations, view the perlpodstyle documentation:

```
[student@OCS student]$ perldoc perlpodstyle
NAME
    perlpodstyle - Perl POD style guide

DESCRIPTION
    These are general guidelines for how to write POD documentation for Perl
    scripts and modules, based on general guidelines for writing good UNIX
    man pages. All of these guidelines are, of course, optional, but
    following them will make your documentation more consistent with other
    documentation on the system.
{remaining output omitted}
```

Additional resources

In each chapter, resources are provided to provide the learner with a source for more information. These resources may include downloadable source code or links to other books or articles that will provide you more information about the topic at hand.

Resources for this chapter can be found here:

`https://github.com/apress/advanced-perl-programming`

Lab exercises

Use POD to document the module that you created in the Chapter 8 lab.

CHAPTER 11

Advanced Features

There is always "a little bit more" that you can learn about any programming language. This chapter is a collection of features that don't necessarily belong in any specific chapter of this book or any of the previous books in the series, but are still very useful to know.

Note The theme of this chapter is "a collection of different topics that were not covered in any previous chapter or book from this series". As a result, you may find the topics skip around randomly!

Perl development environments

Which platform/derivative/tool(s) that you use to code Perl can have an impact on your development process? In some cases, you might not have a choice as to which platform or derivative of Perl you will use to develop your code. However, if you do have a choice, you should spend some time learning the differences between your options.

*nix/Windows

*nix refers to any UNIX-based OS (including Linux). Many developers prefer this environment over Windows for several reasons, including

- UNIX-based systems typically have more powerful features for developers. For instance, most UNIX-based systems have a C or C++ compiler, making it easier to install CPAN modules. Windows systems typically don't have a C/C++ compiler by default.

- UNIX-based systems tend to be more stable than Window-based systems.

© William "Bo" Rothwell of One Course Source, Inc. 2020
W. "Bo" Rothwell, *Advanced Perl Programming*, https://doi.org/10.1007/978-1-4842-5863-7_11

There are other advantages (and some would argue there are advantages of Windows over *nix). Consider the pros and cons of each before deciding your development platform.

In either case, if you are worried about writing portable code, you probably want to review the following document:

`http://perldoc.perl.org/perlport.html`

The perlport document contains useful information regarding writing portable Perl code. It highlights components of Perl that may not be very portable and provides suggestions on how to overcome these potential problems.

Which derivative for *nix?

If you decide to develop on a UNIX-based platform, you may want to consider which derivative of Perl to install and develop on. Unless you want to create a custom build of Perl (well beyond the scope of this book*), your choice will likely come down to two: the standard Perl derivative (`www.perl.org`) or ActiveState's ActivePerl (`www.activestate.com/activeperl`).

When you consider which derivative to use, take the following into account:

- Most *nix systems have Perl installed by default as several system tools (especially on Linux) make use of Perl to manipulate data. In these cases, you are likely to find the standard Perl installed (or a custom build for that Linux distribution).

- ActivePerl comes with a tool to easily install Perl modules: **ppm**. This tool is normally considered easier to use than installing CPAN modules with the **-MCPAN** option.

- ActivePerl's **ppm** doesn't install modules directly from CPAN, but rather from another repository that ActiveState maintains. This means you have access to a subset of the CPAN modules, not the complete set. Note: You can choose additional repositories by clicking `"Edit"` ➤ `"Preferences"` and choosing the `"Repositories"` tab.

---

*If you do want to create your own custom Perl derivative, you probably want to start by looking at the following website: **http://search.cpan.org/dist/App-perlbrew/**.

Which derivative for Windows?

If you are working on a Window's platform, you have a few choices available, as described on www.perl.org:

- **ActiveState Perl** has binary distributions of Perl for Win32 (and Perl for Win64).

- **Strawberry Perl** – A 100% Open Source Perl for Windows that is exactly the same as Perl everywhere else; this includes using modules from CPAN, without the need for binary packages (see http://strawberryperl.com/).

- **DWIM Perl for Windows** – A 100% Open Source Perl for Windows, based on Strawberry Perl. It aims to include as many useful CPAN modules as possible. It even comes with Padre, the Perl IDE (see http://dwimperl.com/windows.html).

A few things to consider:

- ActivePerl has **ppm**, Strawberry Perl does not. However, Strawberry Perl has many CPAN modules installed by default, which can be considered both a pro and a con. The advantage is that you may not need to download and install many new CPAM modules. The disadvantage is there might be way more modules than you would ever need.

- With ActivePerl you can get official support. Strawberry Perl provides only community support.

- Strawberry Perl comes with **gcc**, a C/C++ compiler, making it easier to install modules from CPAN.

- Strawberry Perl release cycle tends to be slower than ActivePerl.

- "When I'm on Windows, I use Strawberry Perl". —Larry Wall

Pick your Perl development tools

There are several good tools to help you develop your Perl code. This includes debuggers, editors, and IDEs. Some of these tools are free, some can be very expensive. Many of them are community supported, while a few are commercially supported.

A good place to start exploring these tools is the following website: www.perlmonks.org/?node_id=531175.

A couple of notes on development tools:

- The PerlMonks link provided earlier hasn't been updated recently, but consider it just a starting point on your journey to find the perfect development tool.

- Specific development tools are not covered in this book because the author really would like you to explore and find what works for you. Not everyone needs or wants a full IDE, and a tool that might work well for the author might not suite your needs. Additionally, development tools are often platform specific, so you really need to find the tool that works on your operating system.

The power of the **do** statement

Often overlooked, the **do** statement is packed with powerful features. The **do** statement was introduced in the *Beginning Perl Programming* book. A quick review of that introduction is provided here.

The idea behind a **do** statement is to execute the statements first and then perform the conditional check:

```perl
#!perl
#do-1.pl
#Verify number entered is greater than 100

do {
    print "Please enter a number greater than 100: ";
    $number=<STDIN>;
} while ($number <= 100);

print "Thanks, $number is greater than 100\n";
```

Either **while** or **until** can be used with a **do** statement to perform the conditional check.

Loop control with do

Important note   The **do** statement is not a loop, even though it may act like one. Loop control statement, like **next** and **last**, cannot be used directly with a **do** statement.

However, there are techniques that you can use to get the functionality of **next** and **last** within a **do** statement. For **next**, you need to create a second set of brackets:

```
do { {
    print "Please enter a number greater than 100: ";
    $number=<STDIN>;
    next if (cond);
} } while ($number <= 100);
```

For **last**, you need to make use of a label:

```
LABEL: {
    do {
        print "Please enter a number greater than 100: ";
        $number=<STDIN>;
        last LABEL if (cond);
    } while ($number <= 100);
}
```

Note   Labels were also introduced in the *Beginning Perl Programming* book.

Sourcing code

Earlier in this book, creating Perl modules was demonstrated. Sometimes creating a module is a bit overkill when you simply want to embed code from another Perl script into your program (often called "sourcing").

One technique that you can use to source code is to use the **eval** statement:

```
eval `cat script.pl`;
```

There are several potential problems with this technique. To begin with, it will only work on Linux- and UNIX-based systems as the **cat** command doesn't exist on Windows-based systems (on Windows systems, the **type** command displays files).

Instead of using the **eval** statement, you can source code using the **do** statement:

```
do "script.pl";
```

There are several differences between the **eval** and **do** technique, even though they are both attempting to perform the same task. The **do** statement doesn't run any external command, which means it won't be platform specific and you don't have to worry about an external command failing.

Additionally, the **do** statement won't have access to scoped variables, but using eval will provide this access. For example, consider the following code:

```
#!perl
#test-1.pl

print "var is $var\n";
```

When executed in another program using the **eval** statement, the **my** variable from the original program is available to the test-1.pl script. See the following example code:

```
#!perl
#eval-1.pl

my $var=100;

eval `type test-1.pl`;
```

And note the execution that was performed on a Windows system:

```
ocs% perl eval-1.pl
var is 100
```

In the next example, the **do** statement is used instead of the **eval** statement:

```
#!perl
#do-2.pl

my $var=100;

do "test-1.pl";
```

Notice that when executed, no value is printed for the $var variable because the **my** variable is not available in the test-1.pl code:

```
ocs% perl do-2.pl
var is
```

Some additional differences between **do** and **eval**:

- The **do** statement will use the paths provided by **@INC** while **eval** will not (it will use regular system paths).

- The **do** statement will update the **%INC** variable, so you can see where the source file was loaded from.

- If the **do** statement can't access the file, it returns **undef** and sets **$!** to the error message (see **do-3.pl** in the following for an example).

- If the **do** statement can access the file, but can't compile the code, it returns **undef** and sets **$@** to the error message (see **do-4.pl** in the following for an example).

- If the **do** statement can compile the code, it returns the outcome of the last statement of the source file.

The following code attempts to load the mytestfile.pl script, which doesn't exist:

```
#!perl
#do-3.pl

do "mytestfile.pl" || print "$!";
```

The following output demonstrates how the $! variable was populated:

```
ocs% perl do-3.pl

No such file or directory
```

The following code attempts to load the test-2.pl script, which fails to compile correctly:

```
#!perl
#do-4.pl

use lib ".";
do "test-2.pl" || print "This is our error: $@";
```

The following output demonstrates how the $@ variable was populated:

ocs% **perl do-4.pl**

This is our error: Can't find string terminator ' " ' anywhere before EOF at test-2.pl line 4.

An additional feature of the **do** statement

The **do** statement also allows you to create simple, inline blocks of code. Consider the following:

$data=do { local $/; <>};

The **do** statement has its own scope, so **local** and **my** variables will only exist in the **do** block.

autodie

The **autodie** pragma provides an easy way to exit your program when a system call fails. This can make the process of debugging code easier.

The **autodie** pragma, available from Perl 5.12, provides an easy way to automatically exit (**die**) from your program if specific functions return false. These functions include those that create system calls and are normally associated with I/O operations.

In its simplest form, **autodie** works like the following:

```
#!perl
#autodie-1.pl

use autodie;

open ($fh, "<", "junkfile");

print "this should not print\n";
```

The following output of autodie-1.pl demonstrates how this pragma performs:

ocs% **perl autodie-1.pl**
Can't open 'junkfile' for reading: 'No such file or directory' at autodie-1.pl line 6

By default, **autodie** will have your program **die** when one or more Perl functions return failure. You can specify which functions you want to have **die** occur automatically by writing code like this:

use autodie qw(open close);

Or you can specify categories:

use autodie qw(:filesys):

The ":filesys" category would include the following Perl functions:

- chdir
- closedir
- opendir
- link
- mkdir
- readlink
- rename
- rmdir
- symlink
- unlink

To see additional categories, consult the **autodie** documentation. Note that when not specified, **autodie** uses the ":default" category, not the ":all" category.

autodie scope

As with most pragmas, you can turn off **autodie** with the **no** statement:

no autodie;

The **autodie** pragma is also scoped, so you can turn it off (or on) for portions of your program by using blocks:

use autodie;   #turns on for :default

#code here

```perl
{
no autodie(:filesys);    #turns off for just :filesys
#code here
}

#code here                #back to :default
```

Using **eval** with **autodie**

When you wrap an **autodie** statement inside an **eval** statement, the program won't die automatically, but rather it sets the **$@** variable with the reason why it might have died:

```perl
#!perl
#autodie-2.pl

use autodie;

eval {open ($fh, "<", "junkfile");};

print "This is why it failed: $@\n";
```

The following demonstrates autodie-2.pl in action:

```
ocs% perl autodie-2.pl
This is why it failed: Can't open 'junkfile' for reading: 'No such file or
directory' at autodie-2.pl line 6
```

Why not use Fatal?

According to the documentation on Fatal: "Fatal has been obsoleted by the new autodie pragma". With that said, you will still see many programmers use the Fatal module. In fact, you will most likely see the Fatal module more often than the autodie pragma, especially in legacy scripts. The main reason why you should avoid using the Fatal module in the future is simply that the Perl developers have tagged it as obsolete in favor of the autodie pragma.

Humorous **autodie** side note

From the **autodie** documentation:

> "bIlujDI' yIchegh()Qo'; yIHegh()!
>
> It is better to die() than to return() in failure.
>
> -- Klingon programming proverb."

String variables as files

Using file operators on data contained in scalar variables provides more flexibility in dealing with string variable data.

As of Perl 5.6, you can open filehandles that either read or write to scalar variables. For example, consider the following code:

```perl
#!perl
#string-1.pl

$data =
"These are the times
in which all men must
rise to the challenge
that this nation now faces
";

open $str_fh, '<', \$data;

$info=<$str_fh>;                    #reads first line
print "$info\n";

read ($str_fh, $input, 5);          #reads next five characters
print "$input\n";

print tell $str_fh, "\n";
seek ($str_fh, 0, 0);               #goes to beginning of $str_fh
print tell $str_fh, "\n";
```

The following output demonstrates how string-1.pl behaves. Note that the operations being used are normally reserved for files, but can now apply to the string data:

```
ocs% perl string-1.pl
These are the times

in wh
25
0
```

You can also open a filehandle that writes to a string, as shown in the following program:

```
#!perl
#string-2.pl

open $str_fh, '>', \$data;

print $str_fh "These are the times\n";
print $str_fh "in which all men must\n";

print "$data\n\n";

close $str_fh;

open $str_fh, '>>', \$data;

print $str_fh "rise to the challenge\n";
print $str_fh "that this nation now faces\n";

print "$data";
```

The following output demonstrates how string-2.pl behaves:

```
ocs% perl string-2.pl
These are the times
in which all men must

These are the times
in which all men must
rise to the challenge
that this nation now faces
```

File::Spec

Dealing with filenames in a script that is supposed to be cross-platform transportable can be a challenge. File::Spec will make this easier.

The built-in module **File::Spec** provides you with several functions that will make it easier to deal with files on different platforms.

Note   This module can be used as either an OO-based module or a procedural module (using functions instead of methods). For this book, procedural examples will be given. To use procedurally, load **File::Spec::Functions** rather than **File::Spec**.

There are many functions available from this module. This section will describe just a few (as described by the **File::Spec** documentation):

- **catdir** – Concatenate two or more directory names to form a complete path ending with a directory. But remove the trailing slash from the resulting string, because it doesn't look good, isn't necessary, and confuses OS/2. Of course, if this is the root directory, don't cut off the trailing slash. ☺

- **catfile** – Concatenate one or more directory names and a filename to form a complete path ending with a filename.

- **curdir** – Return a string representation of the current directory.

- **tmpdir** – Return a string representation of the first writable directory from a list of possible temporary directories. Return the current directory if no writable temporary directories are found. The list of directories checked depends on the platform; for example, File::Spec::Unix checks $ENV{TMPDIR} (unless taint is on) and /tmp.

The following program provides some examples of these File::Spec::Functions:

```perl
#!perl
#filespec1.pl

use File::Spec::Functions;
use File::Spec::Functions qw(tmpdir);
```

197

```
@dir=qw(/ usr share dict);
$file="linux.words";

print catdir(@dir), "\n";
print catfile(@dir, $file), "\n";

print curdir, "\n";
print tmpdir, "\n";
```

Output of filespec1.pl on a Windows-based system:

```
ocs% perl filespec1.pl
\usr\share\dict
\usr\share\dict\linux.words
.
C:\Users\bo\AppData\Local\Temp
```

Output of filespec1.pl on a Linux-based system:

```
ocs% perl filespec1.pl
/usr/share/dict
/usr/share/dict/linux.words
.
/tmp
```

■ **Note**   There is also a CPAN module called **Path::Class** that provides some additional cross-platform filename functionality; however, it was last updated in 2012. You might still find it useful, so if you want to learn more about this CPAN module, go to the following URL:

http://search.cpan.org/dist/Path-Class-0.26/lib/Path/Class.pm

---

Proper use of soft references

Using soft references correctly can result in some handy shortcut techniques.

Earlier in this book in Chapter 2, we introduced references. During that discussion, you learned about the potential problem of soft (or symbolic) references. The following is a brief review of what was covered in that chapter in regard to soft references:

Suppose you execute the following two statements:

```
DB<1> $name="Bob"
DB<2> $$name="Ted"
```

In this example, you ask Perl to assign the value "Ted" to the variable that the scalar variable $name refers to. However, $name doesn't refer to anything... it is set to a scalar value "Bob".

In this case, like many in Perl, Perl tries to make due with the information that you provided and generate the most reasonable result. The `result: Perl` creates a scalar variable called $Bob that is assigned the value "Ted":

```
DB<1> $name="Bob"
DB<2> $$name="Ted"
DB<3> print $Bob
Ted
```

This process is called `"symbolic references"`.

Typically, you want to avoid symbolic references. Not only are they confusing, but they can cause additional problems. It is easy to accidentally make a symbolic reference when you really intended to make a hard reference.

To avoid making symbolic references by accident, use the **use strict 'refs'** statement:

```
#!perl
#strict1.pl

use strict 'refs';

$name="Bob";
$$name="Ted";
```

The following example output of strict.pl demonstrates how the **use strict 'refs'** statement results in errors when symbolic references are used:

```
ocs% perl strict.pl
```
Can't use string ("Bob") as a SCALAR ref while "strict refs" in use at
./strict.pl line 7.

■ **Note**   You can allow symbolic references later in your script by using the
following statement:

no strict 'refs';

Based on the information from the preceding pages, it would seem like soft
references are a "bad thing". When incorrectly used, soft references can cause
problems. However, when correctly used, they can make for clever coding techniques.

Consider a situation in which we need to store values that will represent monthly
sales amount for a given year. To provide more flexibility with the data, we want to store
the data into an array. The first element will represent January, the second element will
represent February, and so on.

We are writing the code to create this array. Initially, we write the code like this:

```perl
sub create_array {
    @data=@_;           #values are passed into sub as arguments
    #some data checking code goes here
    return (@data)
}
```

There are a few potential problems with this technique:

- This technique requires the user to pass in parameters in a specific
  order (January sales first, then February, etc.).

- When the programmer calls this subroutine, there is no easy way to
  "see" what the numbers correspond to: **&create_array("12000",
  "13500", "10200", "4500");**

- There is no way to "skip a month".

It might be better to have the programmer call your program using this technique:

&create_array(January => "12000", February => "13500", April => "10200");

You can change your subroutine to read the parameters into a hash:

```
sub create_array {
    %para=@_;            #values are passed into sub as arguments
    #convert hash into array
    #some data checking code goes here
    return (@data)
}
```

But, how can we convert the hash into an array? We could make some ugly
if-then-else statement:

```
foreach (keys %para) {
    if ($key eq "January") {
        $data[0] = $para{$key};
    } elsif ($key eq "February") {
        $data[1] = $para{$key};
    }
    #more else statements needed here
}
```

While this will work (after writing ten more **elsif** statements), it isn't the best
technique.

Using soft references would be better:

```
$JANUARY    = 0;
$FEBRUARY   = 1;
$MARCH      = 2;
$APRIL      = 3;
$MAY        = 4;
$JUNE       = 5;
$JULY       = 6;
$AUGUST     = 7;
$SEPTEMBER  = 8;
$OCTOBER    = 9;
$NOVEMBER   = 10;
$DECEMBER   = 11;
```

```
sub create_array {
   %para=@_;            #values are passed into sub as arguments
   #convert hash into array:
      for (keys %para) {
          $months[$$_]=$para{$_};
      }
   #some data checking code goes here
   return (@data)
}
```

To understand this, you need to understand how the following line works:

> $months[$$_]=$para{$_};

Suppose **$_** is set to "MARCH". Perl will replace **$_** in $$_ with MARCH, resulting in $MARCH. The value of $MARCH is 2, so $$_ returns a value of 2.

As a result, $month[2] is set to the value of $para{$_} (or $para{MARCH} in this case).

There is, however, a possible concern here. What if someone modifies the variables that we are using ($MARCH, etc.)?

You may be tempted to make the month variables **my** variables. Unfortunately, this won't do the trick. Symbolic references don't "look" at **my** variables, only variables that belong in the package's namespace.

Consider the following code fragment:

```
my $MARCH = 2;
$_=MARCH;
$months{$$_]=.99;
```

When $$_ is evaluated, Perl looks for a reference called $MARCH in the main package symbolic table. Since there isn't a variable called $MARCH in the main symbolic table, Perl returns 0 (since we are using this in a numeric situation). Therefore, you just assigned ".99" to $months [0], not $months [2] like you wanted to do.

So, we can't protect our month variables with **my**. We do have a couple of additional techniques available:

1. Make the month variables "constants"; for instance, you can make them references to a scalar values. For example:

    ```
    *MARCH=\2;
    ```

This technique will generate an error message if someone attempts to modify the $MARCH variable.

2. Don't use variables; use subroutines that return the appropriate value. For example:

```
sub MARCH {return (2);}
```

The code that uses the subroutine would look a little different:

```
for (keys %para) {
    $months[&$_]=$para{$_};
}
```

This technique may be even better since very few programmers will ever attempt to overwrite a subroutine in the Perl module.

Install modules from **CPAN** without admin privileges

In some environments, you can't install modules from CPAN because you don't have administrative rights. However, with the technique described here, you can install these modules.

In an earlier chapter, you learned that you can install CPAN modules using the **-MCPAN** option to Perl:

```
ocs% perl -MCPAN -e 'CPAN::install(Path::Class)'
```

Unfortunately on many systems, this will fail because the installation directory requires administration rights (e.g., root access of UNIX/Linux-based systems). The solution is to use the **local::lib** module:

```
ocs% perl -MCPAN -Mlocal::lib -e 'CPAN::install(Path::Class)'
```

This module will install CPAN modules in another directory which doesn't require admin privileges. By loading **local::lib** in your program, that directory will be accessible when you load additional modules:

```
#!perl

use local::lib;
use Path::Class;
```

Bootstrapping

If you think about **local::lib** logically, you will probably see the problem: in order to install modules, you need **local::lib**. But, since local::lib is not normally installed by default, in order to install **local::lib**, you need to be able to install modules.

You can ask someone with admin rights to install **local::lib**; however, that defeats the purpose of the module (although it would mean that you only need to ask for one module to be installed, not each time you need to install a new module).

The solution is a technique called "bootstrapping" which is described in detail in **local::lib**'s documentation:

http://search.cpan.org/dist/local-lib/lib/local/lib.pm#The_bootstrapping_
technique

After reading the local::lib documentation, you might just consider asking an administrator to install local::lib for you. While it isn't rocket science, there are several steps involved.

Basic testing

You want to perform some basic testing, in other words, determine if something returns true or false. For this, an if statement might be a bit too much work. You can use Test::Simple to perform this task more easily.

Consider the following scenario: you are troubleshooting some code and you want to perform some simple tests on a fragment of code. So, you write the following:

```
if ($data > 1000) {
    print "true 1\n";
}
if ($date eq "1/1/13") {
    print "true 2\n";
}
if ($mark =~ /NULL/) {
    print "true 3\n";
}
```

The previous code could have been done more simply by using the built-in module
Test::Simple:

```
#!perl
#test-simple1.pl

use Test::Simple tests => 3;

$data=999;
$date="1/1/13";
$mark="The Code is NULL";

ok ($data > 1000);
ok ($date eq "1/1/13");
ok ($mark =~ /NULL/);
```

The first line is designed to load the module and specify how many tests we plan to run.

The **ok** function will run the test. If the return value is "true", then the **ok** function
will print "ok" and the test number. If the return value is "false", then the **ok** function
will print "not ok" and the test number. See the following for sample output.

Output of test-simple1.pl:

```
ocs% perl test-simple1.pl
1..3
not ok 1
#   Failed test at test-simple1.pl line 10.
ok 2
ok 3
# Looks like you failed 1 test of 3.
```

If you have a lot of tests, it might be hard to find where the failed tests are by a
numeric value. To make it easier to find them, give them a name:

```
#!perl
#test-simple2.pl

use Test::Simple tests => 3;

$data=999;
$date="1/1/13";
$mark="The Code is NULL";
```

```
ok ($data > 1000, FIRST);
ok ($date eq "1/1/13", SECOND);
ok ($mark =~ /NULL/, THIRD);
```

Output of test-simple2.pl:

```
ocs% test-simple2.pl
1..3
not ok 1 - FIRST
#   Failed test 'FIRST'
#   at test-simple2.pl line 10.
ok 2
ok 3
# Looks like you failed 1 test of 3.
```

Advanced testing

The Test::More module has additional features that Test::Simple lacks. Like **Test::Simple**, **Test::More** is a built-in module that you can use to run tests within your script. It is loaded in a similar manner as well:

```
use Test::More tests => 3;
```

However, it has more features than **Test::Simple**. For example, it isn't always possible to know how many tests you will run. So, **Test::More** has an alternative technique to tell the module that your testing is complete, the done_testing function:

```
use Test::More;

#running tests...

done_testing();
```

The **ok** function is available in **Test::More** and works like **Test::Simple**. Additional functions include the following:

- The **is** function performs an **eq** test operation between the first two arguments.

- The **isnt** function performs an **ne** test operation between the first two arguments.

- The **like** function compares the first argument to a regex pattern match, testing for positive match.

- The **unlike** function compares the first argument to a regex pattern match, testing for negative match.

- The **use_ok** function will attempt to load a module and verify that it loaded correctly (this must be run within a BEGIN block).

Note that this isn't a complete list. Consult the documentation (http://perldoc. perl.org/Test/More.html) for additional tests.

The following provides an example of the Test::More module:

```perl
#!perl
#test-more1.pl

use Test::More;

BEGIN {use_ok ("Text::Wrap", qw (wrap $columns))}
BEGIN {use_ok ("Text::Tabs", qw (tabulate))}

$date="1/1/13";
$mark="The Code is NULL";

is ($date, "1/1/13", SECOND);
like ($mark, qr/NULL/, THIRD);

done_testing();
```

Output of test-more1.pl:

```
ocs% perl test-more1.pl
ok 1 - use Text::Wrap;
not ok 2 - use Text::Tabs;
#   Failed test 'use Text::Tabs;'
#   at test-more1.pl line 7.
#     Tried to use 'Text::Tabs'.
#     Error:  "tabulate" is not exported by the Text::Tabs module
# Can't continue after import errors at (eval 5) line 2
# BEGIN failed--compilation aborted at (eval 5) line 2.
ok 3 - SECOND
```

```
ok 4 - THIRD
1..4
# Looks like you failed 1 test of 4.
```

Using prove

If you write a lot of test scripts, **prove** will make the output (and execution) more functional.

Perl provides the **prove** command which you can use as a "wrapper" program to test scripts. For example:

```
ocs% prove test-more1.pl
test-more1.pl .. 1/?
#   Failed test 'use Text::Tabs;'
#   at test-more1.pl line 7.
#     Tried to use 'Text::Tabs'.
#     Error:  "tabulate" is not exported by the Text::Tabs module
# Can't continue after import errors at (eval 5) line 2
# BEGIN failed--compilation aborted at (eval 5) line 2.
# Looks like you failed 1 test of 4.
test-more1.pl .. Dubious, test returned 1 (wstat 256, 0x100)
Failed 1/4 subtests

Test Summary Report
-------------------
test-more1.pl (Wstat: 256 Tests: 4 Failed: 1)
  Failed test:  2
  Non-zero exit status: 1
Files=1, Tests=4,  1 wallclock secs ( 0.06 usr +  0.06 sys =  0.13 CPU)
Result: FAIL
```

If you run the **prove** command without any filename argument, it runs tests on all files. By default, the **prove** command expects to look for test scripts under a subdirectory called "t" and expects the scripts to have a ".t" extension. If this directory doesn't exist or if there are no files that end with ".t", you will get an error message:

ocs% **prove**

No tests named and 't' directory not found at C:/Perl/lib/App/Prove.pm line 518

So, if you place all of your tests under a directory called "t" and have all of the filenames end in ".t", **prove** will run all of them:

```
ocs% prove
t\test-more1.t .... 1/?
#   Failed test 'use Text::Tabs;'
#   at t\test-more1.t line 7.
#     Tried to use 'Text::Tabs'.
#     Error:  "tabulate" is not exported by the Text::Tabs module
# Can't continue after import errors at t\test-more1.t line 7.
# BEGIN failed--compilation aborted at t\test-more1.t line 7.
# Looks like you failed 1 test of 4.
t\test-more1.t .... Dubious, test returned 1 (wstat 256, 0x100)
Failed 1/4 subtests
t\test-simple1.t .. 1/3
#   Failed test at t\test-simple1.t line 10.
# Looks like you failed 1 test of 3.
t\test-simple1.t .. Dubious, test returned 1 (wstat 256, 0x100)
Failed 1/3 subtests
t\test-simple2.t ..
t\test-simple2.t .. 1/3 #   Failed test 'FIRST'
#     at t\test-simple2.t line 10.
# Looks like you failed 1 test of 3.
t\test-simple2.t .. Dubious, test returned 1 (wstat 256, 0x100)
Failed 1/3 subtests

Test Summary Report
-------------------
t\test-more1.t   (Wstat: 256 Tests: 4 Failed: 1)
  Failed test:  2
  Non-zero exit status: 1
t\test-simple1.t (Wstat: 256 Tests: 3 Failed: 1)
  Failed test:  1
```

```
  Non-zero exit status: 1
t\test-simple2.t (Wstat: 256 Tests: 3 Failed: 1)
  Failed test:  1
  Non-zero exit status: 1
Files=3, Tests=10,  1 wallclock secs ( 0.03 usr +  0.00 sys =  0.03 CPU)
Result: FAIL
```

Useful prove options

You may find the following **prove** options to be useful:

- **--shuffle** – Shuffles the order of the tests so the execution order isn't always the same.

- **-j** – Has the tests run "in parallel" to perform tests quicker.

- **--state** – Remembers previous tests for later comparison. There are many flags for this option, such as "save" which records the status of the tests and "failed" which only runs the tests that failed during the last **prove** run.

Additional test modules

If **Test::Simple**, **Test::More**, and the **prove** command peaked your interest, you should explore their documentation in greater detail. In addition, you might want to look at the following built-in modules (as described in the Perl module documentation):

- **Test** – Provides a simple framework for writing test scripts

- **Test::Builder** – Back end for building test libraries

- **Test::Builder::Module** – Base class for test modules

- **Test::Builder::Tester** – Tests testsuites that have been built with Test::Builder

- **Test::Builder::Tester::Color** – Turns on color in Test::Builder::Tester

- **Test::Harness** – Runs Perl standard test scripts with statistics

Benchmarking

If you are trying to figure out which technique is quicker, use the Benchmark module.

The **Benchmark** module helps you perform benchmarking tasks on your code. It provides many features that you can make use of, including

- **new** – Returns the current time
- **timediff** – Returns the difference between two times
- **timestr** – Converts times into "understandable" formats
- **timeit** – Runs a chunk of code once
- **timethis** – Runs a chunk of code several times
- **timethese** – Runs several chunks of code several times

Note that Benchmark is an OO-based module. This may result in some unusual looking code (unless you understand OO Perl).

See the following for an example:

```perl
#!perl
#bench1.pl
use Benchmark qw(timethese);
open (DATA, "<foiadoc.txt") || die;
@data = <DATA>;
timethese(
    1000,
    {
        test1 => q{
            foreach (@data) {
            my ($match) = m/^(\w+) (\w+)/;
            }
        },
        test2 => q{
            foreach (@data) {
            my ($match) = m/^\w+ (\w+)/;
            }
        },
    }
);
```

211

The following demonstrates the execution of the bench1.pl script:

```
ocs% perl bench1.pl
Benchmark: timing 1000 iterations of test1, test2...
    test1: 156 wallclock secs (155.64 usr +  0.00 sys = 155.64 CPU)
    @  6.43/s (n=1000)
    test2: 127 wallclock secs (126.78 usr +  0.00 sys = 126.78 CPU)
    @  7.89/s (n=1000)
```

As you can see, just adding one additional, unnecessary parenthesis match can have a significant impact when large chunks of data are parsed.

The first argument to the **timethese** function specifies how many times to run each test. The rest of the arguments are in the form of "key-value" pairs in which the key is the name you give the text and the value is a string that contains a block of code to execute for that test.

Note that you can also use subroutine references for the code to execute. See the following code for an example:

```perl
#!perl
#bench2.pl

use Benchmark qw(timethese);
open (DATA, "<foiadoc.txt") || die;
@data = <DATA>;

sub test1 {
    foreach (@data) {
    my ($match) = m/^(\w+) (\w+)/;
    }
}

timethese(
    1000,
    {
        test1 => \&test1,
        test2 => q{
            foreach (@data) {
            my ($match) = m/^\w+ (\w+)/;
```

```
        }
      },
    }
);
```

The following demonstrates the execution of the bench2.pl script:

```
ocs% perl bench2.pl
Benchmark: timing 1000 iterations of test1, test2...
    test1: 54 wallclock secs (54.06 usr +  0.00 sys = 54.06 CPU) @ 18.50/s
    (n=1000)
    test2: 44 wallclock secs (43.67 usr +  0.00 sys = 43.67 CPU) @ 22.90/s
    (n=1000)
```

Basic benchmarking

The following program demonstrates some basic benchmarking using **new**, **timediff**, and **timestr**:

```perl
#!perl
#bench3.pl

use Benchmark qw(timediff timestr);

$time0 = Benchmark->new;

print "please wait...";
for (1..5) {
  sleep rand(5);
}
$time1 = Benchmark->new;
$timed = timediff($time1, $time0);

print "\n\nProgram execution time",timestr($timed),"\n";
```

Output of bench3.pl:

```
ocs% perl bench3.pl
please wait...

Program execution time15 wallclock secs ( 0.00 usr +  0.00 sys =  0.00 CPU)
```

:hireswallclock

If you have the **Time::HiRes** module installed, you can implement more fine-tuned benchmarking by passing **:hireswallclock** when you load the **Benchmark** module:

```
use Benchmark qw(:hireswallclock timethese);
```

The bench4.pl program demonstrates this feature:

```
#!perl
#bench4.pl

use Benchmark qw(:hireswallclock timethese);
open (DATA, "<foiadoc.txt") || die;
@data = <DATA>;

timethese(
    1000,
    {
        test1 => q{
            foreach (@data) {
            my ($match) = m/^(\w+) (\w+)/;
            }
        },
        test2 => q{
            foreach (@data) {
            my ($match) = m/^\w+ (\w+)/;
            }
        },
    }
);
```

See **bench4.pl** for an example:

```
ocs% perl bench4.pl
Benchmark: timing 1000 iterations of test1, test2...
    test1: 151.66 wallclock secs (151.27 usr +  0.00 sys = 151.27 CPU)
    @  6.61/s (n=1000)
    test2: 126.261 wallclock secs (125.98 usr +  0.00 sys = 125.98 CPU)
    @  7.94/s (n=1000)
```

CHAPTER 12

Advanced Data Structures

At some point while writing Perl code (most likely often), you will need to have to deal with large amounts of data. As you likely know, there is always more than one way to perform a task in Perl. That means there is always a "good" way and a "bad" way. Good might mean faster or less memory usage. In any event, this chapter will introduce you to different techniques you can use to deal with data.

Use the Readonly module to create constants

In an earlier chapter, we introduced the built-in Perl pragma "constant.pm", which can be used to create a constant:

```perl
#!perl
#const1.pl

use constant PI => 3.14159;

print "The value of pi is about ", PI, "\n";
```

This technique of creating constants has some disadvantages:

- The constant created by **use constant** is a "constant subroutine." Unfortunately, there are some areas in which subroutines can't be used, like **format** statements and here documents.

- The constant created by **use constant** is not block scoped. If you want to have a constant for a portion of your program (and you don't want to use packages), this technique won't provide that feature.

- While you can create constant lists with **use constant**, it is hard to "see" that they are lists based on their names.

- You cannot create constant hashes with **use constant**.

© William "Bo" Rothwell of One Course Source, Inc. 2020
W. "Bo" Rothwell, *Advanced Perl Programming*, https://doi.org/10.1007/978-1-4842-5863-7_12

The CPAN module **Readonly** provides you with an easy way to create constants that are either scalar, list, or hash structures:

```perl
#!perl
use Readonly;

Readonly $PI => 3.14159;
Readonly @names => ("Smith", "Jones", "Rothwell");
Readonly %cities => ("San Diego" => "CA", "Boston" => "MA");
```

The constants created by Readonly don't have the disadvantages that the constants created by **use constant** have. However, there is a drawback to Readonly constants that you should consider, as described by the documentation provided by the module:

> *Readonly.pm does impose a performance penalty. It's pretty slow. How slow? Run the benchmark.pl script that comes with Readonly. On my test system, "use constant", typeglob constants, and regular read/write Perl variables were all about the same speed, and Readonly.pm constants were about 1/20 the speed.*

> *However, there is relief. There is a companion module available, Readonly::XS. If it is installed on your system, Readonly.pm uses it to make read-only scalars much faster. With Readonly::XS, Readonly scalars are as fast as the other types of variables. Readonly arrays and hashes will still be relatively slow. But it's likely that most of your Readonly variables will be scalars.*

Make large numbers more readable

Consider the following code:

```perl
$data1 = 23459384092784923424;
$data2 = 324234850394234;
$data3 = 2349583095837450372094534;
```

Large numbers in Perl are very difficult to read because of the lack of commas between "thousands" places. However, you can use a feature in Perl to make them more readable:

```
$data1 = 23_459_384_092_784_923_424;
$data2 = 324_234_850_394_234;
$data3 = 23_495_830_958_374_503_720_945_324;
```

Notes:

- The underscore character doesn't change the value of the variables; it just makes it easier to read the data.

- Do not put quotes around the rvalue. As a string, 100_000 is "100_000", not 100,000.

- You can use this on floating point numbers as well: 123.000_000_001.

- As of Perl 5.8, you can use the _ after every two characters: 10_10_10.

Make use of Scalar::Util

The built-in module **Scalar::Util** provides several subroutines that allow you to perform scalar manipulation tasks easier. Note that if you just load the module, no subroutines will be imported; you need to specify which subroutines you want to import into your program.

The following sections cover a couple of the different functions that are available with the **Scalar::Util** module.

dualvar

The **dualvar** function allows you to assign a variable that can act both as a number and as a string:

```
DB<1> use Scalar::Util qw(dualvar)
DB<2> $value = dualvar (10, "ten")
DB<3> print $value + 5
15
DB<4> print $value . " is the value"
ten is the value
```

looks_like_number

The **look_like_number** function returns true if the scalar variable appears to have a numeric value:

```
DB<1> use Scalar::Util qw(looks_like_number)
DB<2> $var1=100
DB<3> $var2="$var2="this is 100"
DB<4> print "yes" if (looks_like_number($var1))
yes
DB<5> print "yes" if (looks_like_number($var2))
```

Note   There are other functions provided by **Scalar::Util**. Consult the documentation to learn about these other functions.

Make use of List::Util

The built-in module **List::Util** provides several subroutines that allow you to perform list manipulation tasks easier. Note that if you just load the module, no subroutines will be imported; you need to specify which subroutines you want to import into your program.

The following sections cover a few of the different functions that are available with the **List::Util** module.

first

The **first** function will look in a list and return the first element that matches a search criterion:

```
DB<1> use List::Util qw(first);
DB<2> @colors=qw(red blue green yellow purple teal black orange brown)
DB<3> $first = first {/^b/} @colors
DB<4> print $first
blue
```

The criterion is fairly flexible. For example, the following will return any value that is greater than the ASCII value of "mauve":

```
DB<5> $first = first {$_ gt "mauve"} @colors
DB<6> print $first
red
```

max, maxstr, min, and minstr

The **max** function will return the highest numerical value of a list, while **maxstr** will return the highest ASCII value of a list. The **min** function will return the lowest numerical value of a list, while **minstr** will return the lowest ASCII value of a list:

```
DB<1> use List::Util qw(max maxstr min minstr)
DB<2> @colors=qw(red blue green yellow purple teal black orange brown)
DB<3> @numbers=1..10
DB<4> print max (@numbers)
10
DB<5> print min (@numbers)
1
DB<6> print maxstr (@colors)
yellow
DB<7> print minstr (@colors)
black
```

reduce

You can use the **reduce** function to perform operations on each "set" of elements:

```
DB<1> use List::Util qw(reduce);
DB<2> @colors=qw(red blue green yellow purple teal black orange brown)
DB<3> $total = reduce { $a . ":" . $b } @colors
DB<4> print $total
red:blue:green:yellow:purple:teal:black:orange:brown
```

The preceding example starts by grabbing the first two elements of @colors, assigning them to $a and $b. It then performs the operation specified by the first argument ({$a . ":" . $b }) and takes the result and assigns that to $a. Then it grabs the third element of @colors, assigns it to $b, and again performs the concatenation operation.

This is repeated until all elements have been operated on. The result is assigned to $total.

Warning $a and $b are assigned as references. If you change the value of these variables, you are really making changes to the corresponding elements in the array.

---

shuffle

The **shuffle** function will return a randomly ordered list:

```
DB<1> use List::Util qw(shuffle);
DB<2> @colors=qw(red blue green yellow purple teal black orange brown)
DB<3> @colors=shuffle(@colors)
DB<4> print "@colors"
black blue brown orange teal red yellow purple green
DB<5> @colors=shuffle(@colors)
DB<6> print "@colors"
green blue red teal purple black brown yellow orange
```

sum

The **sum** function will return a total of the numeric values of a list:

```
DB<1> use List::Util qw(sum);
DB<2> @numbers=1..10
DB<3> print sum (@numbers)
55
```

Make use of List::MoreUtils

The CPAN module **List::MoreUtils** provides you with subroutines that can be used to manipulate lists. This module is designed to supplement the subroutines provided by **List::Util**.

This module provides a huge list of functions. The following is a summary of these functions, as described in the documentation for **List::MoreUtils**:

- **any BLOCK LIST** – Returns a true value if any item in LIST meets the criterion given through BLOCK. Sets $_ for each item in LIST in turn. Returns false otherwise, or if LIST is empty.

- **all BLOCK LIST** – Returns a true value if all items in LIST meet the criterion given through BLOCK, or if LIST is empty. Sets $_ for each item in LIST in turn. Returns false otherwise, or if LIST is empty.

- **none BLOCK LIST** – Logically the negation of any. Returns a true value if no item in LIST meets the criterion given through BLOCK, or if LIST is empty. Sets $_ for each item in LIST in turn. Returns false otherwise.

- **notall BLOCK LIST** – Logically the negation of all. Returns a true value if not all items in LIST meet the criterion given through BLOCK. Sets $_ for each item in LIST in turn. Returns false otherwise, or if LIST is empty.

- **true BLOCK LIST** – Counts the number of elements in LIST for which the criterion in BLOCK is true. Sets $_ for each item in LIST in turn.

- **false BLOCK LIST** – Counts the number of elements in LIST for which the criterion in BLOCK is false. Sets $_ for each item in LIST in turn.

- **firstidx BLOCK LIST** or **first_index BLOCK LIST** – Returns the index of the first element in LIST for which the criterion in BLOCK is true. Sets $_ for each item in LIST in turn. Returns –1 if no such item could be found.

- **lastidx BLOCK LIST** or **last_index BLOCK LIST** – Returns the index of the last element in LIST for which the criterion in BLOCK is true. Sets $_ for each item in LIST in turn. Returns –1 if no such item could be found.

- **insert_after BLOCK VALUE** LIST – Inserts VALUE after the first item in LIST for which the criterion in BLOCK is true. Sets $_ for each item in LIST in turn.

- **insert_after_string STRING VALUE LIST** – Inserts VALUE after the first item in LIST which is equal to STRING.

- **apply BLOCK LIST** – Applies BLOCK to each item in LIST and returns a list of the values after BLOCK has been applied. In scalar context, the last element is returned. This function is similar to map but will not modify the elements of the input list.

- **before BLOCK LIST** – Returns a list of values of LIST up to (and not including) the point where BLOCK returns a true value. Sets $_ for each element in LIST in turn.

- **before_incl BLOCK LIST** – Same as before but also includes the element for which BLOCK is true.

- **after BLOCK LIST** – Returns a list of the values of LIST after (and not including) the point where BLOCK returns a true value. Sets $_ for each element in LIST in turn.

- **after_incl BLOCK LIST** – Same as after but also includes the element for which BLOCK is true.

- **indexes BLOCK LIST** – Evaluates BLOCK for each element in LIST (assigned to $_) and returns a list of the indexes of those elements for which BLOCK returned a true value. This is just like grep, only that it returns indexes instead of values.

- **firstval BLOCK LIST** or **first_value BLOCK LIST** – Returns the first element in LIST for which BLOCK evaluates to true. Each element of LIST is set to $_ in turn. Returns undef if no such element has been found.

- **lastval BLOCK LIST** or **last_value BLOCK LIST** – Returns the last value in LIST for which BLOCK evaluates to true. Each element of LIST is set to $_ in turn. Returns undef if no such element has been found.

- **pairwise BLOCK ARRAY1 ARRAY2** – Evaluates BLOCK for each pair of elements in ARRAY1 and ARRAY2 and returns a new list consisting of BLOCK's return values. The two elements are set to $a and $b.

- **each_array ARRAY1 ARRAY2 ...** – Creates an array iterator to return the elements of the list of arrays ARRAY1, ARRAY2, throughout ARRAYn in turn. That is, the first time it is called, it returns the first element of each array; the next time, it returns the second element; and so on, until all elements are exhausted.

- **mesh ARRAY1 ARRAY2 [ARRAY3 ...]** or **zip ARRAY1 ARRAY2 [ARRAY3 ...]** – Returns a list consisting of the first element of each array, then the second, then the third, and so on, until all arrays are exhausted.

- **uniq LIST** or **distinct LIST** – Returns a new list by stripping duplicate values in LIST. The order of elements in the returned list is the same as in LIST. In scalar context, returns the number of unique elements in LIST.

- **minmax LIST** – Calculates the minimum and maximum of LIST and returns a two-element list with the first element being the minimum and the second the maximum.

This is a huge list of functions, and covering all of them isn't a goal for this book. You probably want to take the time to read the documentation for this module to determine which of these functions will be useful to your needs.

As a demonstration, consider the **any** function. It acts like Perl's built-in **grep** function, in that it can be used to determine if an array has an element that matches a pattern:

```
DB<1> use List::MoreUtils qw(any)
DB<2> @colors=qw(red blue green yellow purple teal black orange brown)
DB<3> if (grep (/^b/, @colors)) {print "yes";}
yes
DB<4> if (any {/^b/}, @colors) {print "yes";}
yes
```

The **any** function seems to work just like the **grep** statement, but it has some advantages over **grep**:

- The **grep** function will find all elements that match a pattern. In a conditional statement, this is not wanted as once we find a match, we want to stop searching the list. The **any** function will stop once a match is made. This is an advantage if your array is huge and you just need to know if a specific element appears in array. The **any** function will, on average, be much quicker than the **grep** function.

- The **grep** function is limited to searching for regular expression patterns. With the **any** function, you can use search criteria like `{ $_ < 750 }`, which means "return true if any of the elements in the array are less than 750".

List formatting

This technique is designed to prevent common errors that occur when you add more elements to a list "by hand".

Consider the following code:

```
@colors=("red", "blue", "yellow", "green", "purple", "teal", "orange",
"black");
```

To make this more readable, you could write the preceding code like this:

```
@colors=(
        "red",
        "blue",
        "yellow",
        "green",
        "purple",
        "teal",
        "orange",
        "black"
);
```

The new format is easier to read, but it can cause future problems. Consider what happens when you attempt to add a new color:

```
@colors=(
        "red",
        "blue",
        "yellow",
        "green",
        "purple",
        "teal",
        "orange",
        "black"
        "white"
);
```

The common error here is to forget to add a comma on the line above your new element. This is even more common of an error when you deal with hashes:

```
%cities = (
    "San Diego"      => "CA",
    "Boston"         => "MA"          #need to remember to
                                      #add comma here...
);
```

Fortunately, there is an easy solution: end all of your lists with commas:

```
@colors=(
        "red",
        "blue",
        "yellow",
        "green",
        "purple",
        "teal",
        "orange",
        "black",
);
%cities = (
```

```
    "San Diego"      => "CA",
    "Boston"         => "MA",            #don't need to remember
                                         #to add comma here!
);
```

The extra comma has no impact on the array or hash besides making it easier for you to add a new element.

On a related note...

Most Perl programmers quickly learn when they can leave off "syntactic sugar". In fact, you are often encouraged to not include extra characters when they are not needed. But, in some cases, this isn't a good idea.

Consider the following code:

```
sub test {
    print "this is just a test"
}
```

Perl allows you to drop the semicolon character at the end of a block (or at the end of a program). However, this isn't a good habit to get into. If you decide to add another statement at the end of the block, you have to remember to place a semicolon on the line above your new line... something that you aren't likely to remember.

Omitting the semicolon doesn't provide any benefit except to allow you to be a bit lazy.

Understand slices

Using slices when you should be using elements can cause logical errors in your code. To understand how this can be, it is important to understand the difference between an array and a list. Consider the following code:

```
@colors=("red", "blue", "yellow", "green", "purple", "teal", "orange",
"black");
```

@colors is an array. ("red", "blue", "yellow", "green", "purple", "teal", "orange", "black") is a list. The terms are not interchangeable, even though they seem like the same thing.

A list is a collection of scalar data. An array is a variable that holds a list.

The difference between an array and a list is subtle. In some cases, they may behave the same. For example, if you assign an array to another array, a list is returned for the rvalue:

```
DB<1> @colors=("red", "blue", "yellow", "green", "purple", "teal", "orange");
DB<2> @hue=@colors
DB<3> print "@colors"
red blue yellow green purple teal orange
DB<4> print "@hue"
red blue yellow green purple teal orange
```

However, assignment to a scalar is a different story. If you assign an array to a scalar, it returns the number of elements in the array. If you assign a list to a scalar, it returns the last element of the list:

```
DB<1> @colors=("red", "blue", "yellow", "green", "purple", "teal", "orange")
DB<2> $hue=@colors
DB<3> print $hue
7
DB<4> $hue=("red", "blue", "yellow", "green", "purple", "teal", "orange")
DB<5> print $hue
orange
```

A slice is a portion of an array, commonly used like this:

```
DB<1> @colors=("red", "blue", "yellow", "green", "purple", "teal", "orange");
DB<2> @hue=@colors[2..4]
DB<3> print "@hue"
yellow green purple
```

An element is a single value of an array, commonly used like this:

```
DB<1> @colors=("red", "blue", "yellow", "green", "purple", "teal", "orange");
DB<2> $hue=$colors[2]
DB<3> print $hue
yellow
```

However, you will sometimes notice Perl programmers use a slice when they should be using an element:

```
DB<1> @colors=("red", "blue", "yellow", "green", "purple", "teal", "orange");
DB<2> $hue=@colors[2]
DB<3> print $hue
yellow
```

which works in this case because a slice is a "sub list" of the array and, when assigned to a scalar, a list returns the last value in the list. Since there is only one value, using a slice in a situation like this doesn't pose any problems.

However, there are situations where you don't want to use slices. Consider the following:

```
DB<1> @data=<STDIN>
red
blue
green
yellow
DB<2> print @data
red
blue
green
yellow
```

And compare it to the following:

```
DB<1> @data[0]=<STDIN>
red
blue
green
yellow
DB<2> print @data
red
```

When you assign to a slice, the slice only sets one value and discards the rest.

Make use of Hash::Util

The built-in module **Hash::Util** provides several subroutines that allow you to perform hash manipulation tasks easier. Note that if you just load the module, no subroutines will be imported; you need to specify which subroutines you want to import into your program.

The following sections describe some of the more commonly used function provided by the **Hash::Util** module.

lock_keys, unlock_keys, and lock_keys_plus

The **lock_keys** function allows you to specify which keys are permitted for a hash. You can turn this feature off by using the **unlock_keys** function:

```
DB<1> use Hash::Util qw(lock_keys unlock_keys lock_keys_plus)
DB<2> %cities=("San Diego" => "CA", "Boston" => "MA")
DB<3> lock_keys(%cities)
DB<4> $cities{"Alanta"}="GA"
Attempt to access disallowed key 'Alanta' in a restricted hash at (eval5)
[C:/Perl/lib/perl5db.pl:638] line 2.
DB<5> $cities{"Boston"}="CA"
```

When you use the **lock_keys** function, you can either have it use the current keys or specify the value keys as an argument:

```
DB<1> use Hash::Util qw(lock_keys unlock_keys lock_keys_plus)
DB<2> @keys=("San Diego", "Boston")
DB<3> lock_keys(%cities, @keys)
DB<4> %cities=("San Diego" => "CA", "Boston" => "MA")
DB<5> $cities{"Alanta"}="GA"
Attempt to access disallowed key 'Alanta' in a restricted hash at (eval 16)
[C:/Perl/lib/perl5db.pl:638] line 2.
DB<6> $cities{"Boston"}="CA"
```

If you want to use the existing keys and specify other legal keys, you can use the **lock_keys_plus** function:

```
DB<1> use Hash::Util qw(lock_keys unlock_keys lock_keys_plus)
DB<2> %cities=("San Diego" => "CA", "Boston" => "MA")
DB<3> @keys=("Alanta", "New York")
DB<4> lock_keys_plus (%cities, @keys)
DB<5> $cities{"Alanta"}="GA"
DB<6> $cities{"Boston"}="CA"
```

lock_value and unlock_value

As specified in the documentation:

> Locks and unlocks the value for an individual key of a hash. The value of a locked key cannot be changed.

Example:

```
lock_value (%cities, "San Diego);
```

lock_hash and unlock_hash

As specified in the documentation:

> lock_hash() locks an entire hash, making all keys and values read-only. No value can be changed, no keys can be added or deleted.

> unlock_hash() does the opposite of lock_hash() . All keys and values are made writable. All values can be changed and keys can be added and deleted.

hash_unlocked

As specified in the documentation:

> Returns true if the hash and its keys are unlocked.

legal_keys, hidden_keys, and all_keys

The **legal_keys** function will return a list of which keys are legal for the hash. Note: This does not mean that a value has been set for the keys, just that the keys are legal keys for the hash.

The **hidden_keys** function will return a list of which keys are legal for the hash, but that are not currently set.

The **all_keys** function will populate two arrays: the first with a list of valid keys and the second with a list of hidden keys.

Take a look at the following example that illustrates these functions:

```perl
#!perl
#keys1.pl

use Hash::Util qw(lock_keys_plus legal_keys hidden_keys all_keys);

%cities=("San Diego" => "CA", "Boston" => "MA");
@keys=("Alanta", "New York");
lock_keys_plus (%cities, @keys);

$"="\n";

@legal=legal_keys(%cities);
print "Legal\n-----\n", "@legal\n\n\n";

@hidden=hidden_keys(%cities);
print "Hidden\n------\n", "@hidden\n\n\n";

all_keys(%cities, @set, @hidden);
print "Set\n---\n", "@set\n\n\n";
print "Hidden\n------\n", "@hidden\n";
```

Note the output of keys1.pl:

```
ocs% perl keys1.pl
Legal
-----
San Diego
Boston
New York
Alanta
```

```
Hidden
------
New York
Alanta

Set
---
San Diego
Boston

Hidden
------
New York
Alanta
```

Make use of Hash::MoreUtils

The CPAN module **Hash::MoreUtils** provides you with subroutines that can be used to manipulate hashes. This module is designed to supplement the subroutines provided by **Hash::Util**.

This module provides several functions. The following is a summary of these functions, as described in the documentation for **Hash::MoreUtils**:

- **slice HASHREF[, LIST]** – Returns a hash containing the (key, value) pair for every key in LIST

- **slice_def HASHREF[, LIST]** – Same as slice, but only includes keys whose values are defined

- **slice_exists HASHREF[, LIST]** – Same as slice, but only includes keys which exist in the hashref

- **slice_grep BLOCK, HASHREF[, LIST]** – Same as slice, with an arbitrary condition

- **hashsort [BLOCK,] HASHREF** – Returns the (key, value) pairs of the hash, sorted by some property of the keys; by default (if no sort block given), sorts the keys with **cmp**

- **safe_reverse [BLOCK,] HASHREF** – Returns safely reversed hash (value, key pairs of original hash)

Take a look at the following example that illustrates these functions:

```perl
#!perl
#MoreUtils1.pl

use Hash::MoreUtils qw(slice slice_def slice_exists slice_grep);

%ext=qw      (Bob   x1234                      Sue   x1111
             Brian x1233                       Ted   x8878
             Bill x1234);

undef $ext{Brian};
%b= slice \%ext, Bob, Bill, Brian, Steve;
while (($person, $phone) = each (%b)) {print "$person\t$phone\n"}
print "------\n";

%b= slice_def \%ext, Bob, Bill, Brian, Steve;
while (($person, $phone) = each (%b)) {print "$person\t$phone\n"}
print "------\n";

%b= slice_exists \%ext, Bob, Bill, Brian, Steve;
while (($person, $phone) = each (%b)) {print "$person\t$phone\n"}
print "------\n";

%b= slice_grep {/^[BT]/} \%ext;
while (($person, $phone) = each (%b)) {print "$person\t$phone\n"}
print "------\n";

@order=hashsort \%ext;
print "@order\n";
```

The output of MoreUtils1.pl demonstrates these features:

```
ocs% perl MoreUtils1.pl
Steve
Brian
Bob     x1234
Bill    x1234
------
Bob     x1234
```

233

```
Bill     x1234
------
Bill     x1234
Brian
Bob      x1234
------
Ted      x8878
Bill     x1234
Bob      x1234
Brian
------
Bill x1234 Bob x1234 Brian  Sue x1111 Ted x8878
```

Smart use of subscripts

Overuse of subscripts in arrays and hashes can have a performance impact on your program. Array "lookups" are slower than looking up data from a scalar, and hash "lookups" are even slower.

So, how should this potential problem be solved? This section covers several techniques that you can utilize.

Example #1 – Avoid array subscripts

Consider the following code:

```
@colors=qw(red blue green yellow purple pink black brown);
for $i (0..$#colors) {print "colors[$i]\n";}
```

And compare it to the following code:

```
@colors=qw(red blue green yellow purple pink black brown);
for $i (@colors) {print "$i\n";}
```

There are two primary reasons why the second technique is better than the first:

1. It is faster because array lookups take more time (see **sub-bench1.pl** in the following for a demonstration).

2. It is easier to read.

The sub-bench1.pl program:

```perl
#!perl
#sub-bench1.pl

use Benchmark qw(timethese);

@colors=qw(red blue green yellow purple pink black brown);

timethese(
    10000000,
    {
        test1 => q{
            for $i (0..$#colors) {print TEST "$colors[$i]\n";}
            },
        test2 => q{
            for $i (@colors) {print TEST "$i\n";}
            }
    }
);
```

Execution of sub-bench1.pl demonstrates the difference between the speed of the two techniques:

```
ocs% perl sub-bench1.pl
Benchmark: timing 10000000 iterations of test1, test2...
    test1:  9 wallclock secs ( 8.14 usr +  0.00 sys =  8.14 CPU)
    @ 1228350.33/s (n=10000000)
    test2:  8 wallclock secs ( 7.25 usr +  0.00 sys =  7.25 CPU)
    @ 1379310.34/s (n=10000000)
```

You might be thinking "the difference is only 1 second" and that does seem trivial. But, this was a very small array (although many operations of a very small array). Larger arrays will result in even larger time differences. And even if it is only a second, why choose a slower technique that provides no other advantages?

Example #2 – Avoid hash subscripts

Hash subscripts are even more expensive of an operation than array subscripts and should be avoided whenever possible. For example, see the following program:

```perl
#!perl
#sub-bench2.pl

use Benchmark qw(timethese);

timethese(
    10000000,
    {
        test1 => q{
            for $key (keys %ENV) {print TEST "$ENV{$key}\n";}
            },
        test2 => q{
            for $value (values %ENV) {print TEST "$value\n";}
            }
    }
);
```

Output of sub-bench2.pl:

```
ocs% perl sub-bench2.pl
Benchmark: timing 10000000 iterations of test1, test2...
    test1: 137 wallclock secs (137.25 usr +  0.00 sys = 137.25 CPU)
    @ 72859.74/s (n=10000000)
    test2: 83 wallclock secs (83.23 usr +  0.00 sys = 83.23 CPU)
    @ 120143.21/s (n=10000000)
```

Example #3 – Proper use of subscript

In some cases, you want to use subscripts. For example, if you are parsing data in an array and want to know what item number you are currently on:

```perl
@colors=qw(red blue green yellow purple pink black brown);

for $i (0..$#colors) {print "$i: colors[$i]\n";}
```

If you are doing this, you want to avoid using the subscript more than once. For example, the following isn't a very efficient technique (the subscript is performed twice):

```
@colors=qw(red blue green yellow purple pink black brown);

for $i (0..$#colors) {
    if ($colors[$i] =~/^b/) {          #first lookup
        print "colors[$i]\n";}         #second lookup
}
```

Since subscripting is an expensive operation, it *might* be better to utilize a temporary variable:

```
@colors=qw(red blue green yellow purple pink black brown);

for $i (0..$#colors) {
    $temp = $colors[$i];
    if ($temp =~/^b/) {
        print "temp\n";}
}
```

To see an example of this, take a look at the following program:

```
#!perl
#sub-bench3.pl

use Benchmark qw(timethese);

timethese(
    10000000,
    {
        test1 => q{
            for $i (0..$#colors) {
                if ($colors[$i] =~/^b/) {
                    print TEST "colors[$i]\n";}
            }
        },
        test2 => q{
            for $i (0..$#colors) {
                $temp = $colors[$i];
```

```
        if ($temp =~/^b/) {
            print TEST "temp\n";}
        }
    }
}
);
```

The execution of this program demonstrates the difference in speed:

```
ocs% perl sub-bench3.pl
perl sub-bench3.pl
Benchmark: timing 10000000 iterations of test1, test2...
    test1: 17 wallclock secs (18.09 usr +  0.00 sys = 18.09 CPU) @
    552669.39/s (n=10000000)
    test2: 20 wallclock secs (19.16 usr +  0.00 sys = 19.16 CPU) @
    522002.40/s (n=10000000)
```

Note   As previously mentioned, this temporary variable solution might be better. This is why benchmarking is useful. Test your situation carefully to see if it is better for the data that you are using.

Understand the advantages and disadvantages of for, foreach, grep, and map

On the surface, it seems pretty straightforward:

- **for** is a traditional C "for" statement, typically too slow when attempting to iterate over elements in an array.

- **foreach** is designed to effectively iterate over elements in an array.

- **grep** is designed to match patterns in the elements of an array and return a list of the elements that matched.

- **map** is designed to perform operations on each element of an array and return a list of the modified elements.

However, there are some cases in which you have a choice as to which of these you could use. This section will focus on specific cases in which one function would be better than another (of course, you always want to use benchmarking to be certain).

To begin with, recall how **grep** and **map** work. The **grep** function is designed to search for a regular expression pattern in an array and return a list of matched value:

```
@colors=qw(red blue green yellow purple pink black brown);

@b = grep (/^b/, @colors);
```

The **map** function is designed to make changes to data in an array, one element at a time, and return a list of the changed data. In this example, the **-s** operator (returns file size) is run on each of the elements in the @filenames array, and the return value of **map** (a list of file sizes) is stored in @filesize:

```
@filesize = map -s, @filenames;
```

You can think of **map** as doing the following:

```
foreach (@filenames) {
    push (@filesize, -s $_);
}
```

The **map** function will automatically use the default variable, **$_**. This variable is also the default for the **-s** operator.

Return based on regular expression matching

Consider the following lines of code:

```
DB<1> @colors=qw(red blue green yellow purple pink black brown);
DB<2> @b = grep (/^b/, @colors);
DB<3> print "@b"
blue black brown
DB<6> @b = map (/^(b.*)/, @colors);
DB<7> print "@b"
blue black brown
```

As you can see, **map** can return what was matched in a pattern (it returns the value of the first parenthesis match). So, for this situation which technique is better, **grep** or **map**?

You should use **grep** if the purpose is to just return match patterns:

- The sole purpose of **grep** is to return elements that match a regular expression pattern. It is more clear what it is doing than **map**.

- For this scenario, **grep** is also normally faster (see **grep-map-bench1.pl**).

Modifying the original array

The **map** function can be used to modify the original array:

```
DB<1> @colors=qw(red blue green yellow purple pink black brown);
DB<2> @b = map s/^b.*/null/, @colors
DB<3> print "@colors"
red null green yellow purple pink null null
```

This is because **$_** isn't a copy of the elements of @colors, but rather a reference of the elements.

You are probably used to using **foreach** to modify elements in an array:

```
DB<1> @colors=qw(red blue green yellow purple pink black brown);
DB<2> foreach (@colors) {s/^b.*/null/;}
DB<3> print "@colors"
red null green yellow purple pink null null
```

The results are the same, but which is better? You want to use **foreach** in this case:

- The **map** function is designed to return a modified version of an array. In the preceding case, the @b array is worthless... we don't need or want it. The **foreach** loop is much more clear.

- However, there is no reason why you need to assign map to anything. And, as you can see by looking at **foreach-map-bench1.pl**, **map** can be faster than **foreach** when the return value of **map** is discarded:

```
#!perl
#foreach-map-bench1.pl

use Benchmark qw(timethese);
```

```
@colors=qw(red blue green yellow purple pink black brown);

timethese(
    10000000,
    {
        test1 => q{
            @b = map s/^b.*/null/, @colors
        },
            test2 => q{
        map s/^b.*/null/, @colors
        },
        test3 => q{
            foreach (@colors) {s/^b.*/null/;}
            }
    }
);
```

Example exccution:

ocs% **perl foreach-map-bench1.pl**

Benchmark: timing 10000000 iterations of test1, test2, test3...
> *test1: 154 wallclock secs (153.08 usr + 0.00 sys = 153.08 CPU) @*
> *65326.17/s (n=10000000)*
> *test2: 18 wallclock secs (18.78 usr + 0.00 sys = 18.78 CPU) @*
> *532453.01/s (n=10000000)*
> *test3: 27 wallclock secs (26.92 usr + 0.00 sys = 26.92 CPU) @*
> *371457.23/s (n=10000000)*

Using substitution to make a modified copy of the original

Consider the output of the following:

```
DB<1> @colors=qw(red blue green yellow purple pink black brown);
DB<2> @b = map s/^b.*/null/, @colors
DB<3> print "@b"
 1    1 1
```

The return of the **map** function is a list of the returns of the substitution. If **/s** performs any substitutions, it returns a numeric value that indicates how many substitutions it performed (1 in the preceding example). If it can't perform any substitutions, it returns a null string for "false".

If you wanted to make a modified copy of the original array, you could use **foreach**:

```
DB<1> @colors=qw(red blue green yellow purple pink black brown);
DB<2> foreach (@colors) {$hue=$_; $hue =~ s/^b.*/null/; push (@b, $hue);}
DB<3> print "@colors"
red blue green yellow purple pink black brown
DB<4> print "@b"
red null green yellow purple pink null null
```

Or, you can use a feature of the **map** function:

```
DB<1> @colors=qw(red blue green yellow purple pink black brown);
DB<2> @b=map { ($hue = $_) =~ s/^b.*/null/; $hue} @colors
DB<3> print "@colors"
red blue green yellow purple pink black brown
DB<4> print "@b"
red null green yellow purple pink null null
```

So, which method is better? In this case, many would argue that the **foreach** loop is more clear/understandable than the **map** statement. And, if you look at **foreach-map-bench2.pl**, you will see that using **foreach** is quicker than using **map**:

```perl
#!perl
#foreach-map-bench2.pl

use Benchmark qw(timethese);

@colors=qw(red blue green yellow purple pink black brown);

timethese(
    1000000,
    {
        test1 => q{
            foreach (@colors) {$hue=$_; $hue =~ s/^b.*/null/; push (@b, $hue);};
        },
```

```
        test2 => q{
            @b=map { ($hue = $_) =~ s/^b.*/null/; $hue} @colors;
            }
    }
);
```

Example execution:

```
ocs% perl foreach-map-bench2.pl
Benchmark: timing 1000000 iterations of test1, test2...
    test1:  3 wallclock secs ( 3.20 usr +  0.25 sys =  3.45 CPU) @
    289603.24/s (n=1000000)
    test2:  4 wallclock secs ( 3.67 usr +  0.03 sys =  3.70 CPU) @
    270124.26/s (n=1000000)
```

Know different sort techniques

In the *Beginning Perl Programming* book, we introduced the **sort** function. The **sort** function will perform an ASCII sort on the elements of an array:

```
DB<1> @arr=("north", "south", "east", "west");
DB<2> @sortarr = sort (@arr);
DB<3> print "@sortarr";
east north south west
```

There are many other "types" of sorts that you can perform. By default, the **sort** function uses **cmp** to perform an ASCII sort, but you can also perform a numeric sort by using the following syntax:

```
DB<1> @num=(10,7,99,93,0);
DB<2> @sortnum=sort {$a <=> $b} (@num);
DB<3> print "@sortnum";
0 7 10 93 99
```

The **$a** and **$b** variables are used by **sort** to perform comparison operations on each element of the array.

You must use **$a** and **$b**; they are special variables in Perl, used specifically for the **sort** function. In fact, their order is also important; put the **$b** variable first and you get a reverse sort:

```
DB<1> @num=(10,7,99,93,0);
DB<2> @sortnum=sort {$b <=> $a} (@num);
DB<3> print "@sortnum";
99 93 10 7 0
```

You can also perform operations on **$a** and **$b** before the sort takes place. A common example is to make a case-insensitive sort by using the **lc** (lowercase) function:

```
DB<1> @arr=("north", "south", "East", "West");
DB<2> @sortarr = sort (@arr);
DB<3> print "@sortarr";
East West north south
DB<4> @sortarr = sort { lc($a) cmp lc ($b) }(@arr);
DB<5> print "@sortarr";
East north south West
```

Customized sorts

The **sort** is a lot more powerful than many Perl programmers realize. For example, suppose you had a list of files in an array and you want to sort them by file size:

```
@by_size=sort { -s $a <=> -s $b } @files;
```

The more complex the **sort**, the more difficult it will be to read it. So, put the sorting technique into a subroutine:

```
DB<1> sub bysize { -s $a <=> -s $b }
DB<2> @files=glob '*.pl'
DB<3> print "@files"
bench1.pl const1.pl file-temp1.pl foreach-map-bench1.pl foreach-map-bench2.
pl grep-map-bench1.pl keys1.pl MoreUtils1.pl scalar-more1.pl sub-bench1.pl
sub-bench2.pl sub-bench3.pl tie-file1.pl
DB<4> @sortfiles=sort bysize @files
DB<5> for (@sortfiles) {print -s $_, "\t$_\n";}
```

56	scalar-more1.pl
99	const1.pl
214	file-temp1.pl
265	tie-file1.pl
304	sub-bench2.pl
329	grep-map-bench1.pl
339	foreach-map-bench1.pl
355	sub-bench1.pl
394	bench1.pl
395	foreach-map-bench2.pl
480	sub-bench3.pl
481	keys1.pl
781	MoreUtils1.pl

If you do place your sort technique into a subroutine, you can use *prototyping* to make use of **$_[0]** and **$_[1]** instead of **$a** and **$b**. This is important if your subroutine is in a different package than the calling program since **$a** and **$b** won't be available in a different package (**$a** and **$b** are special *package* variables, not global throughout the entire program):

```
package Test;
sub bysize {$$} { -s $_[0] <=> -s $_[1] }

package main;
@sortfiles=sort Test::bysize @files;
```

Sort by file modification time

In this example, we will make use of the Perl function stat, which returns data about a file. By default, it returns a list of up to 13 values, including file ownership, file size, and modification times. The tenth value (or ninth if you are thinking in terms of array indexes) contains the date when the file was last modified:

```
DB<1> ($dev,$ino,$mode,$nlink,$uid,$gid,$rdev,$size, \
            $atime,$mtime,$ctime,$blksize,$blocks) = stat("const1.pl")
DB<2> print $mtime
1356584053
```

This time is expressed in the number of seconds since the epoch (Jan 1, 1970) and when the file was last modified.

Of course, we don't need/want the other values in this case, so we can make use of a list trick to just return the one value that we want:

```
DB<1> $mtime = (stat("const1.pl"))[9]
DB<2> print $mtime
1356584053
```

And now we can use the stat function to sort an array of files based on their modification time:

```
DB<1> @files=glob "*.pl"
DB<2> @sortfiles=sort {(stat($a))[9] <=> (stat($b))[9]} @files
```

Hash value sorting

Consider the following situation: you have a hash and you want to return all of the keys in sorted order, but not sorted by the keys, but by their values:

```
DB<1> %test=('a' => 'z', 'b' => 'x', 'c' => 'y')
DB<2> @keys = sort { $test{$a} cmp $test{$b} } keys %test
DB<3> print "@keys"
b c a
```

Complex sorting example

In the following example, taken directly from the documentation for **sort**, you can see how complex you can make **sort**. The following example will "...sort by descending numeric compare using the first integer after the first = sign, or the whole record case-insensitively otherwise":

```
#!perl
#complex-sort1.pl

use feature "fc";   #need v5.16

@old=("code=129", "test=876", "result=563");
```

```perl
my @new = sort {
    ($b =~ /=(\d+)/)[0] <=> ($a =~ /=(\d+)/)[0]
                        ||
                fc($a)  cmp  fc($b)
    } @old;

print "@new\n";

@old=("Red", "Blue", "Green", "brown");

my @new = sort {
    ($b =~ /=(\d+)/)[0] <=> ($a =~ /=(\d+)/)[0]
                        ||
                fc($a)  cmp  fc($b)
    } @old;

print "@new\n";
```

Output of `complex-sort1.pl`:

```
ocs% perl complex-sort1.pl
test=876 result=563 code=129
Blue brown Green Red
```

The Orcish Maneuver

Consider an earlier example:

```perl
@by_size=sort { -s $a <=> -s $b } @files;
```

Because of how **sort** works, this is a pretty ineffective technique. A faster technique would be

```
DB<1> @files=glob '*.pl'
DB<2> @sortfiles=sort { ( $t{$a} ||= -s $a ) <=> ( $t{$b} ||= -s $b ) }
      @files
DB<3> for (@sortfiles) {print -s $_, "\t$_\n";}
56      scalar-more1.pl
99      const1.pl
```

To understand this, first consider what the **||=** operator does. Consider the following code:

$c ||= $d;

This is the same as

$c = $c || $d;

which means "set $c to $c if it is defined, set it to $d if $c is not defined".

In the **sort** example on the previous page, the following means set the hash key of "$a" to the value of $t{$a} if that is set; otherwise, set it to -s $a.

($t{$a} ||= -s $a)

And then it returns that value to be used by the **sort** operation. Why is this faster than the original example? In the original, the **-s** operation is run over and over, often on the same file repeatedly. With the Orcish Maneuver, the outcome of each **-s** operation is "cached" into a hash (%t in our example) and that value is used for the next time **sort** needs that value.

Important note   The hash variable should be empty each time you run this **sort**, so consider placing it within its own block and make it a **my** variable:

```perl
{
my %t;
@sortfiles=sort { ( $t{$a} ||= -s $a ) <=> ( $t{$b} ||= -s $b ) } @files;
}
```

To see how much faster it is than the original technique, look at **orc-bench1.pl**:

```perl
#!perl
#orc-bench1.pl

use Benchmark qw(timethese);

@files=glob '*.pl';
timethese(
    100000,
    {
        test1 => q{
            @by_size=sort { -s $a <=> -s $b } @files;
        },
        test2 => q{
            @sortfiles=sort { ( $t{$a} ||= -s $a ) <=> ( $t{$b} ||= -s $b )
            } @files;
        },
    }
);
```

Example output:

```
ocs% perl orc-bench1.pl
Benchmark: timing 100000 iterations of test1, test2...
    test1: 597 wallclock secs (77.91 usr + 517.75 sys = 595.66 CPU) @
    167.88/s (n=100000)
    test2:  1 wallclock secs ( 0.80 usr +  0.00 sys =  0.80 CPU) @
    125470.51/s (n=100000)
```

Note   The numbers in the previous output are not a typo. The Orcish Maneuver is much, much faster than a normal sort operation.

Avoid using memory to store large data

Large chunks of data can result in memory issues. While it might impact the speed of your code, keeping the data on the hard drive will reduce memory errors.

When dealing with large chunks of data, storing the data in memory can cause problems. While data manipulation might be quicker, RAM becomes full quickly and this could cause your program to crash.

One simple technique to dealing with this is to store data in a file. However, manipulating the data can be challenging. You can read one line at a time, manipulate the line, save the result into a file, and then read another line.

You can also make use of **Tie::File**, a built-in Perl module that will allow you to treat a file like an array. Each line in the file is treated as an element in the tied array. The file is not stored in memory, and changes take place immediately in the file.

See the following for an example:

```perl
#!perl
#tie-file1.pl

use Tie::File;

tie @data, 'Tie::File', "testdata.txt" || die;

print "Number of lines: $#data\n";
print "First line:\n\t$data[0]\n";

$result=shift (@data);
print "Shifted line\n\t$result\n";
print "New first line:\n\t$data[0]\n";
```

Creating temporary files

If you don't need to create permanent data, you can make use of a temporary file by using the **File::Temp** module. This is a Perl built-in module that will create a unique temporary file for you and allow you to write to this file.

```perl
#!perl
#file-temp1.pl
```

```perl
use File::Temp qw(tempfile);

( $fh, $file_name ) = tempfile();

for (keys %ENV) {
print $fh $i++, "\t$_ => $ENV{$_}\n";
}

$fh->close;

rename $file_name => "my-final-file.txt";
```

The file location should be a place on the system in which files are "cleaned up" by the OS.

You can specify a suffix for the temporary file in or have the temporary file placed in a specific directory:

```perl
( $fh, $file_name ) = tempfile(SUFFIX => '.txt');
( $fh, $file_name ) = tempfile(DIR => '/tmp');
```

You can also use **File::Temp** to create temporary directories:

```
DB<1> use File::Temp qw(tempdir)
DB<2> $dir=tempdir
DB<3> print $dir
/tmp/cd_0zveYHq
```

OO nature of File::Temp

The **File::Temp** module can either be used as a procedural module (using functions) as described earlier or as an OO-based module (using method calls). If you have experience with OO-based modules, you can use the following:

```perl
$temp = new File::Temp();
```

You can still write to $temp as a normal filehandle.

CHAPTER 13

New Features

To develop Perl programs correctly, you should understand the versions of Perl that are available and which one you should use. Perl 5.000 was released on October 17, 1994. It was a nearly complete rewrite of Perl 4; however, it was (mostly) backward compatible to Perl 4.

The goal was to create a more efficient language that also had additional useful features. After the release of version 5.000, additional releases were made:

Date	Release
March 13, 1995	5.001
February 29, 1996	5.002
June 25, 1996	5.003
May 15, 1997	5.004
July 22, 1998	5.005

Minor versions (mostly bug fixes and security patches) were also introduced. Those versions were defined by the following notation: 5.005058 or 5.005_58.

The release of the next version of Perl after 5.005 resulted in a different numbering convention:

> When developing Perl 5.6, the decision was made to switch the versioning scheme to one more similar to other open source projects; after 5.005_63, the next version became 5.5.640, with plans for development versions to have odd numbers and stable versions to have even numbers.

It was also at this time when Larry Wall and the Perl community started working on Perl 6 (which is still in development).

© William "Bo" Rothwell of One Course Source, Inc. 2020
W. "Bo" Rothwell, *Advanced Perl Programming*, https://doi.org/10.1007/978-1-4842-5863-7_13

As a result of this naming convention change, versions of Perl that end in an even number (5.6. 5.8, 5.10, etc.) are considered stable releases and odd numbers (5.7, 5.9, 5.11) are development releases, not to be used in production coding.

Additionally, minor releases still occur and are designated release numbers like 5.8.1.

It is important to note that the old naming convention is still commonly used within Perl code. For example, version 5.10.1 can still be referred to as 5.010001 within Perl. This is still possible to allow for numeric comparison operations. Recall the **$]** variable holds the current version of Perl:

```
DB<1> print $]
5.010001
```

Note that as of Perl 5.6, you can also use the **$^V** variable that stores the version of Perl in the "newer" format:

```
DB<1> print $^V
v5.16.1
```

The **$^V** is designed to allow you to use string comparison operations to perform version checking.

Note   To see a more detailed Perl timeline, go to `http://history.perl.org/PerlTimeline.html`.

The latest, greatest?

You should always consider when you use new features; doing so might cause portability issues.

In this book series, we typically don't cover all of the new bells and whistles that are available in newer versions of Perl. There are several reasons for this:

- Often the company/group that you work for mandates an older version of Perl (or just hasn't upgraded to a newer version of Perl).

- If you are trying to write code for other people, using a newer feature might cause problems if they don't have a newer version of Perl that has that feature.

- Perl is (mostly) backward compatible, which means if you know how to write code in Perl 5.6, that code should work just fine in Perl 5.16 (with a few possible exceptions).

This isn't to suggest that you shouldn't use the latest version of Perl. In fact, you probably should consider avoiding older versions of Perl (if you can) for the following reasons:

- Older versions of Perl are not supported or maintained. Typically, only the current and previous stable releases are maintained. Occasionally, some security bugs are fixed for previous versions, but that isn't always the case.

- There are some newer features which are nice to have available (hence the point of this seminar).

So, using the latest version of Perl is considered to be "best practice"; however, using the latest features of Perl can cause problems if others use an older version of Perl to run your code. To limit this potential problem as much as possible, you should always start your programs with a line like the following:

```
require 5.16;
```

If you do this, your program will not execute unless Perl version 5.16 (or higher) is being used to run your code:

```
#perl
#req.pl

require 15.6;

print "This is only a test";
```

Output of req.pl:

```
ocs% perl req.pl
Perl v5.1600.0 required--this is only v5.10.1, stopped at req.pl line 4.
```

Or you can use the **$]** variable to ensure you have the right version of Perl.

The feature pragma

Some new features are added in such a way that you can enable them or leave them disabled.

Starting in Perl 5.10, new features are included via the **use feature** pragma. As the documentation states, "The **feature** `pragma is used to enable new syntax that would break Perl's backwards-compatibility with older releases of the language."`

To make use of a new feature, you use the following syntax:

```
use feature "feature_name";
```

Some of these new features include

- **say** – A replacement for **print** that automatically prints a newline character (5.10+)

- **state** – A replacement for **my** that differs in that it will retain previously set values (5.10+)

- **switch** – Provides a switch statement called **given** (5.10+)

- **unicode_strings** – Tells the compiler to use Unicode semantics in all string operations executed within its scope (5.12+)

- **current_sub** – Provides the **__SUB__** token that returns a reference to the current subroutine or **undef** outside of a subroutine (5.16+)

- **array_base** – Supports the legacy **$[** variable (5.16+)

- **fc** – Tells the compiler to enable the **fc** function, which implements Unicode casefolding

---

Note   As new versions of Perl are introduced, new features will also be added. See `https://perldoc.perl.org/feature.html` to get a full list of all new features.

Example of use feature 'say' and use feature 'state'

The following program demonstrates how the say and state features work:

```
#!perl
#feature-1.pl

use feature 'state';
use feature 'say';

sub show {
    state $var;
    say "The variable is set to $var";
    $var=100;
}

&show;
&show;
```

Output of feature-1.pl:

```
ocs% perl feature-1.pl
The variable is set to
The variable is set to 100
```

The given statement

As of Perl 5.10, the **given** statement is available:

```
use feature "switch";
```

It is slightly confusing that asking for the "switch" feature gives you access to a function called "given"; however, the **given** function acts like a switch statement, as demonstrated by the following program:

```
#!perl
#given1.pl

use feature "switch";   #Provides access to the given statement
```

```perl
print "Please enter 'yes' or 'no': ";
$response=<STDIN>;
chomp $response;

given ($response) {
        when ("yes") {print "You agree!\n"; }
        when ("no")  {print "Bummer, you don't agree\n"; }
        default     {print "Maybe next time\n"; }
}
```

The value "default" is a keyword for **given**. It is used as a "catchall." Keep in mind that once a match is made, no additional conditions will be checked. If you use "default", it should be placed at the bottom of the **given** conditions.

An alternative format for when

As with Perl's **if** statements, you can place the condition before or after **when** (Perl 5.14 and higher):

```perl
#!perl
#given2.pl
#must use v5.14+

use feature "switch";

print "Please enter 'yes' or 'no': ";
$response=<STDIN>;
chomp $response;

given ($response) {
        print "You agree!\n" when "yes";
        print "Bummer, you don't agree\n" when "no";
        default {print "Maybe next time\n"};
}
```

Pattern matches with given

The **given** statement will assign the variable that you provide to **$_**. For example, the $response variable in the following code fragment is assigned to **$_** within the **given** statement:

```
given ($response) {
      print "You agree!\n" when "yes";
      print "Bummer, you don't agree\n" when "no";
      default {print "Maybe next time\n"};
}
```

This means that you can also use regular expression pattern matching (or numeric comparisons) with **given**:

```
given ($response) {
      print "You agree!\n" when /^y/i;
      print "Bummer, you don't agree\n" when /^n/i;
      default {print "Maybe next time\n"};
}
```

The default comparison for given

So, if you don't specify the comparison technique, what exactly is **given** doing? That isn't an easy question to answer. Consider what the documentation (see http://perldoc. perl.org/perlsyn.html) states:

> *Exactly what the EXPR argument to when does is hard to describe precisely, but in general, it tries to guess what you want done. Sometimes it is interpreted as $_ ~~ EXPR, and sometimes it does not. It also behaves differently when lexically enclosed by a given block than it does when dynamically enclosed by a foreach loop. The rules are far too difficult to understand to be described here. See Experimental Details on given and when later on.*

Note that ~~ is "smartmatching" which will be covered later in this chapter.

Given that it is hard to determine exactly what is happening, you may opt to explicitly provide the condition:

```perl
given ($response) {
        when ($_ eq "yes") {print "You agree!\n"; }
        when ($_ eq "no")  {print "Bummer, you don't agree\n"; }
        default     {print "Maybe next time\n"; }
}
```

Using continue with given

As mentioned previously, once a conditional check is matched, the **given** statement executes the corresponding code and then no additional checks are made. However, you can tell **given** to "continue" to check more conditions by using the **continue** statement:

```perl
#!perl
#given3.pl

use feature "switch";  #Provides access to the given statement

print "Please enter 'yes' or 'no': ";
$response=<STDIN>;
chomp $response;

given ($response) {
        when ("yes") {print "You agree!\n"; continue;}
        when ("no")  {print "Bummer, you don't agree\n"; continue;}
        default      {print "Thank you for your response\n"; }
}
```

New foreach technique

When you use the **switch** feature, you can now make use of **when** statements in **foreach** loops:

```perl
#!perl
#foreach1.pl

use feature "switch";
```

```perl
@colors=qw(blue green red yellow red brown red green);

foreach (@colors) {
        when ("red") {print "I see red!\n";;}
        when ("green") {print "I see green!\n";;}
        default      {print "Don't know this color: $_\n"; }
}
```

Using __SUB__

There are times in which you want to recursively call a subroutine. However, this can be difficult when the subroutine name could be changed in future iterations of the program.

The solution is to use __SUB__. Outside of a subroutine, the __SUB__ token will return **undef**. Inside of a subroutine, it will return a reference to the subroutine:

```
DB<1> use feature 'current_sub'
DB<2> print __SUB__
DB<3> sub test {print __SUB__,"\n";}
DB<4> &test
CODE(0x2f916e8)
```

If you want to run the subroutine, use the following code:

```perl
#!perl
#sub1.pl
#Be sure to use 5.16 or higher!

sub loop_it {
   state $var;
   $var++;
   print "The var is now $var\n";
   if ($var <= 5) {__SUB__ ->();}
}

&loop_it;
```

Using all features of a specific Perl version

Both the **say** and **state** features are available in Perl 5.10. To load both features (and all others available in this version), use the following code:

```
#!/usr/local/bin/perl
#feature-2.pl

use 5.010;

sub show {
    state $var;
    say "The variable is set to $var";
    $var=100;
}

&show;
&show;
```

You can also say **use v5.10**.

features are lexically scoped

You can turn on features for specific parts of a program by placing **use feature** in its own scope:

```
#!perl
#feature-3.pl

sub show {
    use feature 'state';
    use feature 'say';

    state $var;
    say "The variable is set to $var";
    $var=100;
}

&show;
&show;
```

You can also turn off features with the **no** statement:

```perl
#!perl
#feature-4.pl

use feature 'state';
use feature 'say';

sub show {

    state $var;
    say "The variable is set to $var";
    $var=100;
}

&show;
&show;

no feature 'say';
#more code here...
```

New option: -E

As of Perl 5.10, there is a new option: **-E**. This option works just like **-e**, but it automatically enables all of the features for the version of Perl being executed.

Make use of the Smartmatch operator

Introduced in Perl 5.10, the Smartmatch operator, ~~, will perform matching of items based on their context. In other words, it behaves differently (polymorphic) depending on the values being compared. It returns true (1) if the match is made and false ("") if the match is not made.

Consider how you currently look for a key in a hash:

```perl
if ( exists $hash{key} ) { }
```

This could also be done with smartmatching:

```perl
if ( $key ~~ %hash) { }
```

Note   Think of ~~ as "in" or "inside of" when you convert this into a verbal expression. For example, you could think of the previous code as "$key is inside of %hash".

Using regex expressions

In the example on the preceding page, there wasn't any difference between using **exists** and ~~. However, what if you wanted to look for a key based on a regular expression:

```
if (%hash ~~ /^A/) {
    print "A key that started with A was found\n";
}
```

The same could be done with an array (although **grep** would have done the trick as well, just not as fast as ~~):

```
if (@array ~~ /^A/) {
    print "A element that started with A was found\n";
}
```

Note   Due to how the Smartmatch operator works, the order of the parameters doesn't matter. In other words, **@array ~~ /^A/** is the same as **/^A/ ~~ @array**.

Additional Smartmatches

You can use Smartmaches to perform other sorts of matching. For example, to find if two arrays have the same elements in the same order:

```
if (@array1 ~~ @array2) { }
```

To see if all of the keys of one hash are the same as another hash:

```
if (%hash1 ~~ %hash2) { }
```

Suppose you had a list of scalars in an array and you want to determine if one of those is a key within a hash:

```
if (%hash ~~ @array) { }
```

Note   You can find more Smartmatch features here: `http://perldoc.perl.org/perlop.html#Smartmatch-Operator`.

The given statement

Smartmatching is often used with the **given** statement. So, to use ~~, you can do the following:

```
#!perl
#given1.pl

use feature "switch";

print "Please enter 'yes' or 'no': ";
$response=<STDIN>;
chomp $response;

given ($response) {
        when ($_ ~~ /^y/) {print "You agree!\n"; }
        when ($_ ~~ /^n/)  {print "Bummer, you don't agree\n"; }
        default    {print "Maybe next time\n"; }
}
```

Recall that ~~ *might* be the default comparison operator for **when**, but this isn't 100% certain, so using ~~ is a good idea.

Use Perl 5.10.1 or higher

Smartmatch was introduced in Perl 5.10. However, it was significantly modified in Perl 5.10.1, so it works differently in 5.10.1 and higher. To make sure your code uses the 5.10.1 version of Smartmatch, make sure the following is in your code:

```
use 5.010001;
```

The // operator

Introduced in Perl 5.10, the // operator provides a handy way of performing the following task:

```
DB<1> print defined $code ? $code : "NULL"
NULL
```

The preceding means check to see if $code is defined, if it is, return that value, otherwise return the value of "NULL":

```
DB<2> $code="A127Z"
DB<3> print defined $code ? $code : "NULL"
A127Z
```

With the // operator, you can simply do the following:

```
DB<4> print $code // "NULL"
A127Z
```

You can also use //= for assignment:

```
DB<5> $code //= "NULL"
DB<6> print $code
A127Z
```

which means "assign $code to NULL if $code is not already defined."

The UNITCHECK block

Introduced in Perl 5.10, the UNITCHECK block provides another level at which you can execute code. Prior to Perl 5.10, there were four blocks that you could utilize outside of the regular execution part of your program:

BEGIN – Executes code immediately, during compile time

CHECK – Executes code immediately after initial compile time

INIT – Executes code immediately before runtime

END – Executes code immediately after runtime

Note that, as of Perl 5.14, you can always tell what block you are in by looking at the value of the **${^GLOBAL_PHASE}** variable.

The **UNITCHECK** block, as described by the documentation:

> **CHECK** and **INIT** blocks, while useful for some specialized
> purposes, are always executed at the transition between the
> compilation and the execution of the main program, and thus are
> useless whenever code is loaded at runtime. On the other hand,
> **UNITCHECK** blocks are executed just after the unit which defined
> them has been compiled.

While many Perl developers know about **BEGIN** and **END** blocks, **CHECK**, **INIT**, and **UNITCHECK** are not as known; however, they can be very useful for debugging Perl code.

In an attempt to make these blocks more clear, the documentation for **perlmod** provides the following code example:

```
#!/usr/bin/perl
# begincheck
print           "10. Ordinary code runs at runtime.\n";
END { print     "16.   So this is the end of the tale.\n" }
INIT { print    " 7. INIT blocks run FIFO just before runtime.\n" }
UNITCHECK {
  print         " 4.   And therefore before any CHECK blocks.\n"
}
CHECK { print   " 6.   So this is the sixth line.\n" }
print           "11.   It runs in order, of course.\n";
BEGIN { print   " 1. BEGIN blocks run FIFO during compilation.\n" }
END { print     "15.   Read perlmod for the rest of the story.\n" }
CHECK { print   " 5. CHECK blocks run LIFO after all compilation.\n" }
INIT { print    " 8.   Run this again, using Perl's -c switch.\n" }
print           "12.   This is anti-obfuscated code.\n";
END { print     "14. END blocks run LIFO at quitting time.\n" }
BEGIN { print   " 2.   So this line comes out second.\n" }
UNITCHECK {
print           " 3. UNITCHECK blocks run LIFO after each file is
compiled.\n"
}
```

```
INIT { print    " 9.    You'll see the difference right away.\n" }
print           "13.    It merely _looks_ like it should be confusing.\n";
__END__
```

Output of begincheck.pl:

ocs% **perl begincheck.pl**

1. *BEGIN blocks run FIFO during compilation.*
2. *So this line comes out second.*
3. *UNITCHECK blocks run LIFO after each file is compiled.*
4. *And therefore before any CHECK blocks.*
5. *CHECK blocks run LIFO after all compilation.*
6. *So this is the sixth line.*
7. *INIT blocks run FIFO just before runtime.*
8. *Run this again, using Perl's -c switch.*
9. *You'll see the difference right away.*
10. *Ordinary code runs at runtime.*
11. *It runs in order, of course.*
12. *This is anti-obfuscated code.*
13. *It merely _looks_ like it should be confusing.*
14. *END blocks run LIFO at quitting time.*
15. *Read perlmod for the rest of the story.*
16. *So this is the end of the tale.*

Small changes in Perl 5.10

The following is a list of small changes to Perl 5.10 that you should be aware of:

- You can now use **chdir**, **chmod**, and **chown** on filehandles, not just filenames.

- The **sort** function now supports recursive sorting.

- The **unpack** and **mkdir** variables now default to using **$_**.

- The **$*** and **$#** variables have been removed.

- The special arrays **@-** and **@+** are no longer interpolated in regular expressions.

- Instead of setting a signal handle key to "DEFAULT" (e.g., **$SIG{INT}=**
  "DEFAULT"), you can **undef** the value or **delete** the key/value pair.

- Pseudo-hashes have been removed.

- Several new modules are available.

See the documentation for further information.

Yada yada

Introduced in Perl 5.12, the "yada yada" operator (...) is a handy way of saying "I need to put some real code here later." For example, you plan on creating a subroutine called "get_data", so to make that clear, you create the following:

```
#!perl
#yada1.pl

sub get_data {

}

&get_data;
```

This creates an "empty" function as a reminder to you to write that function later. The problem with this is that if you forget to write the function, the output of the program doesn't make it clear that the function is missing its code:

```
ocs% perl yada1.pl
```

Instead, you should use the yada operator:

```
#!perl
#yada2.pl
#use perl 5.12 or higher!

sub get_data {
    ...
}

&get_data;
```

Perl will not generate a compile error, but it throws an exception with the text "Unimplemented":

```
ocs% perl yada2.pl
Unimplemented at yada2.pl line 6.
```

The reason why this is useful is that it can prevent logical errors in larger scripts when you thought you wrote the subroutine, but really didn't, and you tried to call it.

Using each, keys, and values with arrays

Introduced in Perl 5.12, the **each**, **keys**, and **values** functions will work on arrays in addition to hashes. Recall the **each** is used on hashes to pull key/value pairs from a hash one at a time:

```
while (($key, $value) = each (%hash)) {print "$key = $value\m";}
```

If you use this technique on an array, **each** will return two values, the index and the element:

```
DB<1> @colors=qw(red blue green yellow)
DB<2> while (($index, $value) = each (@colors)) {print "$index =
$value\n";}
0 = red
1 = blue
2 = green
3 = yellow
```

The previous technique is akin to using a **for** statement to transverse the array:

```
DB<1> @colors=qw(red blue green yellow)
DB<3> for (0..$#colors) {print "$_ = $colors[$_]\n";}
0 = red
1 = blue
2 = green
3 = yellow
```

In most cases, the **for** statement will be for efficient, both in terms of memory and speed. However, if you find yourself doing many array lookups ($colors[$_]) in the **for** loop, you may want to consider using the **each** loop. Array lookups are more expensive than scalar lookups, so benchmarking would be best to determine the best method.

You can also use **keys** and **values** on arrays as of Perl 5.12. The **keys** function returns a list of index values (0, 1, 2, 3 in the preceding example) and **values** returns all of the values of the array.

It seems silly to return all of the keys, except you will find that it is faster to use the second code fragment in the following than the first:

```
for (values @colors) {print "$_ = $colors[$_]\n";}
for (0..$#colors) {print "$_ = $colors[$_]\n";}
```

See the following for a demonstration of the difference between these two techniques:

```
#!perl
#bench-values1.pl

use Benchmark qw(timethese);
@colors=qw(red blue green yellow);

timethese(
    10000000,
    {
        test1 => q{
            for (0..$#colors) {
                        print DUMMY "$_ = $colors[$_]\n";
                }
        },
        test2 => q{
            for (values @colors) {
                        print DUMMY "$_ = $colors[$_]\n";
                }
        },
    }
);
```

Output of bench-values1.pl:

```
ocs% perl bench-values1.pl
Benchmark: timing 10000000 iterations of test1, test2...
    test1: 10 wallclock secs (10.34 usr +  0.00 sys = 10.34 CPU)
    @ 966837.47/s (n=10000000)
    test2:  9 wallclock secs ( 7.80 usr +  0.00 sys =  7.80 CPU)
    @ 1282544.57/s (n=10000000)
```

Small changes in Perl 5.12

The following is a list of small changes to Perl 5.12 that you should be aware of:

- Perl now supports **\N**, a new regex escape which you can think of as the inverse of **\n**.

- The statement **delete local** now allows you to locally delete a hash entry.

- The **use v5.12** (or **use 5.012**) statement enables **strict** by default.

- Several new modules are available.

- The autodie pragma (covered in Chapter 12).

See the documentation for further information.

New regular expression modifiers

Introduced in Perl 5.14, the following four regex modifiers are now available (as described by the documentation):

- The **/l** modifier says to compile the regular expression as if it were in the scope of use locale, even if it is not.

- The **/u** modifier says to compile the regular expression as if it were in the scope of a use feature 'unicode_strings' pragma.

- The **/d** (default) modifier is used to override any use locale and use feature 'unicode_strings' pragmas in effect at the time of compiling the regular expression.

- The **/a** regular expression modifier restricts **\s**, **\d**, and **\w** and the POSIX ([[:posix:]]) character classes to the ASCII range. Their complements and **\b** and **\B** are correspondingly affected. Otherwise, **/a** behaves like the **/u** modifier, in that case-insensitive matching uses Unicode semantics.

Note   Due to the fact that Unicode is outside the scope of this book, examples of these modifiers are not provided. It is important to note that since Perl 5.10, a lot of Unicode support has been implemented in Perl. If you are not familiar with Unicode, a web search for "unicode vs ascii" will provide you with information to start understanding what Unicode is all about.

Nondestructive substation

Introduced in Perl 5.14, the **/r** modifier allows you to perform substation and translation operations without changing the original variable. Instead, the changed string is returned and can be assigned to another scalar variable:

```
DB<1> $line="The dog ate the dog food from the dog bowl"
DB<2> $newline = $line =~ s/dog/cat/gr
DB<3> print $line
The dog ate the dog food from the dog bowl
DB<4> print $newline
The cat ate the cat food from the cat bowl
```

Automating regular expression modifiers

Introduced in Perl 5.14, you can make use of the **re** pragma to specify which modifiers to automatically use with all regex patterns.

Typically, the **/s**, **/m**, and **/x** modifiers are popular modifiers to use with each pattern match. To automate this throughout your program, you can use the following:

```
use re '/smx';
```

You can also turn this off by using **no re**:

```
no re '/smx';
```

This pragma is lexically scoped, so you can enable it for short periods of your program by implementing it within a block:

```
#code without use re here
{
use re '/smx';
#code with use re here
}
#code without use re here
```

New feature for given

Introduced in Perl 5.14, the **given** statement will return the last expression that was evaluated. You can capture this with a **do** statement, as demonstrated in the following example:

```
#!perl
#given-return1.pl

use feature "switch";   #Provides access to the given statement

print "Please enter 'yes' or 'no': ";
$response=<STDIN>;
chomp $response;

$choice = do {
    given ($response) {
        "1" when /^y/i;
        "2" when /^n/i;
        "0" when /.*/;
    }
};

print "$choice\n";
```

Small changes in Perl 5.14

The following is a list of small changes to Perl 5.14 that you should be aware of:

- A package declaration can now contain a code block, in which case the declaration is in scope inside that block only: **package Foo { ... }**.

- A new global variable, **${^GLOBAL_PHASE}**, has been added to allow introspection of the current phase of the Perl interpreter.

- Several new modules are available.

See the documentation for further information.

Change in use feature

Introduced in Perl 5.16 is a change to the way that **use feature** works. Consider the following code:

```
use 5.016;
#some code here
use 5.014;
```

In previous versions of Perl, the second **use** statement would effectively do nothing as the features from version 5.14 were already enabled with the **use 5.016** statement.

In Perl 5.16, the second **use** statement would first disable all features and then enable the features for version 5.14 (and previous).

Additionally, the **use feature** statement will enable strict by default (standard behavior since 5.12), but in Perl 5.16, it will also override **no strict** if the **use feature** statement comes after the **no strict** statement. In versions 5.12 and 5.14, **use feature** would not automatically override **no strict**.

The CORE namespace

Introduced in Perl 5.16, you can now make use of features without explicatively loading them. Features are automatically placed in the **CORE** namespace. As a result, you can make use of them by using a fully qualified package name:

```
DB<1> CORE::say "hello"
hello
```

Many of Perl's standard keywords are also placed in the **CORE** namespace. This allows you to alias these keywords by using typeglobs:

```perl
#!perl
#core1.pl

BEGIN {*addend = \&CORE::push;}

@colors=qw(red blue green);
addend @colors, "purple";
print "@colors\n";
```

As of Perl 5.16, the following keywords are available via **CORE**: **chdir**, **chomp**, **chop**, **each**, **eof**, **exec**, **keys**, **lstat**, **pop**, **push**, **shift**, **splice**, **stat**, **system**, **truncate**, **unlink**, **unshift**, and **values**.

Overriding Perl keywords

Introduced in Perl 5.16, you can now override Perl built-in functions (keywords) by modifying the pseudo-namespace **CORE::GLOBAL**.

Suppose you don't want anyone to use the **chop** statement in your program. You can override it with the following:

```perl
#!perl
#core2.pl

BEGIN {*CORE::GLOBAL::chop = sub {warn "chop not allowed\n";} }

$string="This is a good day to learn Perl.";
chop $string;
```

Small changes in Perl 5.16

The following is a list of small changes to Perl 5.16 that you should be aware of:

- The **current_sub** feature is enabled as of this version.

- The **fc** feature is enabled as of this version.

- The **$$** variable can now be assigned to.

- When **\N{name}** is encountered, the **charnames** module is now automatically loaded when needed.

- Several new modules are available.

See the documentation for further information.

Changes beyond Perl 5.16

At this point you might be thinking, "We are currently using Perl 5.30 (when you read this it might actually be a higher version); are all of the changes in all of the versions going to be covered?" The answer to that is "no" because there are literally hundreds of changes and covering all of them would be a book by itself. The purpose of this chapter wasn't to cover all of the changes in all of the versions, but rather to make you aware of how Perl 5 is a living, growing language, with new features routinely added to the language.

Additionally, as a Perl developer, you want to be aware of what changes occur in which version of Perl. This can be done by either reviewing all of the changes of every version of Perl or by performing unit test of your code using different versions of Perl.

Why should you test your Perl code using different versions? Well, if you are writing code that you are going to share with others, they may not be using the same version of Perl that you are. While it may be uncommon to find a system that is using Perl 5.10 or 5.12 when version 5.30 is available, it isn't completely unheard of. And certainly newer versions, like 5.26 and 5.28, are still widely used.

It is also important to spend a little time looking at the changes when a new version of Perl is released, especially if you upgrade to the new version on your system. This isn't just because you may want to take advantage of the new Perl features, but also because some Perl features are Deprecated, which could end up breaking your code (it shouldn't, because Deprecated really means "no longer recommended to use" and not "no longer available," but sometimes it does). You also should look at the section called Incompatible Changes as that can have an effect on code you wrote on previous versions. As an example, take a look at a snippet of the 5.28.0 Delta documentation:

- Incompatible Changes
  - Subroutine attribute and signature order
  - Comma-less variable lists in formats are no longer allowed
  - The :locked and :unique attributes have been removed
  - \N{} with nothing between the braces is now illegal
  - Opening the same symbol as both a file and directory handle is no longer allowed
  - Use of bare << to mean <<"" is no longer allowed
  - Setting $/ to a reference to a non-positive integer no longer allowed
  - Unicode code points with values exceeding IV_MAX are now fatal
  - The B::OP::terse method has been removed
  - Use of inherited AUTOLOAD for non-methods is no longer allowed
  - Use of strings with code points over 0xFF is not allowed for bitwise string operators
  - Setting ${^ENCODING} to a defined value is now illegal
  - Backslash no longer escapes colon in PATH for the -S switch
  - the -DH (DEBUG_H) misfeature has been removed
  - Yada-yada is now strictly a statement
  - Sort algorithm can no longer be specified
  - Over-radix digits in floating point literals
  - Return type of unpackstring()
- Deprecations
  - Use of perlfunc/vec EXPR,OFFSET,BITS on strings with code points above 0xFF is deprecated
  - Some uses of unescaped "{" in regexes are no longer fatal
  - Use of unescaped "{" immediately after a "(" in regular expression patterns is deprecated
  - Assignment to $[will be fatal in Perl 5.30
  - hostname() won't accept arguments in Perl 5.32
  - Module removals

So, the real lessons for this chapter are

- Read the Deltas (changes in Perl versions) to learn about new Perl features.

- If you use a new feature, make sure you document which version of Perl uses that feature and consider using a **require** statement to enforce that version (or higher) of Perl.

- Read the Deltas to discover what Perl features are Deprecated or Incompatible with older Perl code.

All new features are documented on the following URL: `https://perldoc.perl.org/5.30.0/index-history.html`.

Index

© William "Bo" Rothwell of One Course Source, Inc. 2020
W. "Bo" Rothwell, *Advanced Perl Programming*, https://doi.org/10.1007/978-1-4842-5863-7

Printed in the United States
By Bookmasters

Printed in the United States
By Bookmasters